ASSURANCE IN THE N

New Testament believers were assured, and were so right from the time of their conversion. Yet many believers today lack assurance. Why is this?

According to the later Puritans, while assurance is possible and desirable, believers have to struggle long and hard for it, looking to their sanctification to see if they have sufficient evidence for it; most, however, will struggle in vain. And since this teaching still dominates the Reformed and evangelical world (most of which is unaware of the source of the trouble), it is exacting a heavy price – not only making many believers anxious, but legalistic.

And herein lies the key to the question posed above. David Gay shows, from Scripture, that when believers listen to misguided or false teaching, they get into bondage and lose their joy. It happened in New Testament days. But the apostles dealt with it, writing to these believers to reassure them. Sadly, however, assurance-by-sanctification teachers compound the problem for many by taking this apostolic teaching and turning it on its head, thereby reinforcing their bondage and sadness. Gay traces the problem to the root; namely, the preaching of sanctification under the law instead of the gospel, and making that sanctification the way of assurance. Hence the grief so many believers suffer today.

Gay has written his book to help such anxious believers back to Scripture and to the joy of their salvation. Many have gone astray because they have begun with experience (this experience being governed by the legal system in which they are locked), and forced Scripture to fit it. This is wrong. As Gay does here, we must always start with Scripture, and then come to experience.

So if you are concerned about the subject of assurance, this book is for you. Gay wants you to read it with an open Bible, as a Berean (Acts 17:11). If you find that his teaching does not stand the scrutiny of Scripture, reject it. But if you find biblical truth in what you read here, accept it and live on it – whatever the cost. Cost? Some, at least, who cling to the legal assurance-by-sanctification system, will not be slow in dismissing you as arrogant, an antinomian, a deluded mystic, or whatever. You have been warned!

All books
by David H.J.Gay
are available on
Amazon Books and Kindle

Free Mobi and Epub downloads
are available in 'Links' at
David H J Gay Ministry (sermonaudio.com)

Free pdf downloads
are available on
archive.org and openlibrary.org

Assurance
in
The New Covenant

And the disciples were filled with joy and with the Holy Spirit

Acts 13:52

David H.J.Gay

BRACHUS

BRACHUS 2014
davidhjgay@googlemail.com

Scripture quotations, unless otherwise stated,
are from the New International Version

ABBREVIATIONS
New International Version: NIV
New King James Version: NKJV
Authorised or King James Version: AV
New American Standard Bible: NASB
Good News Bible: GNB

A well-grounded assurance [makes a man] the most active worker in the field, the most valiant warrior in the battle, and the most patient sufferer in the furnace! There are none as active as the assured!... If God should say to your soul: 'I am your salvation', and if you [knew]... that you were a child of God, do you think it would make you unholy? Do you think it would make you negligent? No, I think I see the tears in your eyes, as you reply: 'I would do anything for him; I would live for him; I would die for him, to show how I love him who loved me'. Ah, poor soul, if you believe in Christ now, that will be true! If you will cast yourself on Jesus now, you shall be forgiven! There shall be no sin left in God's book against you; you shall be absolved, acquitted, delivered, cleansed and washed. And then you shall prove in your experience that assurance does not make men sin, but that assurance of pardon is the very best means of making men holy, and keeping them in the fear of God!...

There is a certain breed of Calvinists, whom I do not envy, who are always jeering and sneering as much as they can at the full assurance of faith. I have seen their long faces; I have heard their whining periods, and read their dismal sentences in which they say something to this effect: 'Groan in the Lord always, and again I say, groan! He who mourns and weeps, he who doubts and fears, he who distrusts and dishonours his God, shall be saved'. That seems to be the sum and substance of their very un-gospel-like gospel!... Notice that David would not be satisfied unless his assurance had a divine source. 'Say unto my soul' [Ps. 35:3]...

Nothing short of a divine testimony in the soul will ever content the true Christian. The Spirit of God must himself, after a supernatural sort, speak to our consciences, and to our hearts. Gracious God!... speak yourself, with your word of truth, and wisdom, and say to me, even to me: 'I am your salvation!'

Charles Haddon Spurgeon[1]

---

[1] 'Full Assurance' (sermon number 384).

Contents

Note to the Reader

New Testament believers enjoyed a far higher level of assurance and consequent joy than the majority of believers do today. This is not only sad: it ought not to be. And I want to do what I can about it. But realising that I might be misunderstood, I must set the record straight right from the start.

I am *not* saying that an unassured believer is not a believer. As I will explain, true believers can lose their assurance – especially when living in the ambience of poor or misguided teaching. Not only 'can'; many do! And one of my main purposes in writing is to help these unassured believers recover (or find) the joy of their salvation.

Having said that, I have a narrow path to tread. I don't want to give any *unbeliever* a sense of assurance. Quite the opposite. Until the sinner trusts Christ, he is under the wrath and condemnation of God, is on the high road to perdition, and, unless he comes to Christ, he will eternally perish. Consequently I hope my words will disturb, alarm and awaken all such – before it is too late!

Nor do I want to give assurance to any professing believer who pleads he is 'a carnal Christian', citing 1 Corinthians 3:1-4 as his excuse. Such a professor abuses the apostle's words. Paul was rebuking the Corinthians – not congratulating them! If, reader, you are hiding behind a misuse of the apostle's words, I want to disturb you – not lull you to sleep!

Furthermore, I am *not* saying that the believer is sinlessly perfect, or has no trials, doubts, afflictions, temptations or struggles. Nor am I saying that sanctification is of no consequence. I have just shown what I think of the 'carnal Christian'! A believer must be sanctified. A believer will be sanctified. Sanctification is no option: 'Without holiness no one will see the Lord' (Heb. 12:14). 'God... has saved us and called us to a holy life' (2 Tim. 1:8-9). A believer must keep Christ's commands (John 14 – 16). And he will: 'If anyone is in Christ, he is a new creation; the old has gone, the new has come!' (2 Cor. 5:17). 'I urge you to live a life worthy of the calling you have received... So I tell you this, and

9

insist on it in the Lord, that you must no longer live as the Gentiles do' (Eph. 4:1,17). And take John:

If we claim to have fellowship with him yet walk in the darkness, we lie and do not live by the truth... We know that we have come to know him if we obey his commands. The man who says: 'I know him', but does not do what he commands is a liar, and the truth is not in him. But if anyone obeys his word, God's love is truly made complete in him. This is how we know we are in him: whoever claims to live in him must walk as Jesus did... If anyone says: 'I love God', yet hates his brother, he is a liar. For anyone who does not love his brother, whom he has seen, cannot love God, whom he has not seen. And he has given us this command: whoever loves God must also love his brother (1 John 1:5; 2:3-6; 4:20-21).[1]

Moreover, we, as believers, can weigh the testimony of others only by the evidence we see (or do not see) in their lives. Sanctification, I say again, is no option!

I make all this clear right at the start so as to forestall any misunderstanding in what is to follow.

I do not pretend that this small book is a learnèd tome on the doctrine of assurance. Not at all! It must not be bracketed with, for instance, Thomas Brooks' 320 pages, Joel R.Beeke's 412 pages, John Owen's several volumes, or Michael A.Eaton's more than 700 pages on the subject.[2] And the contrast lies in more than page count. I am aiming for a very different audience. Without intending any patronisation, I want to produce a little work that is accessible, simple, and therefore useful to the 'ordinary' believer, something that might serve at least as an introduction to a very important

---

[1] See also Rom. 12 – 16; Eph. 4 – 6, for instance.

[2] Thomas Brooks: *Heaven on Earth: A Serious Discourse, Touching a Well-Grounded Assurance* in *The Works of Thomas Brooks*, The Banner of Truth Trust, Edinburgh, 1980, Vol.2 (also in paperback, 1961, 320 pages); Joel R.Beeke: *The Quest for Full Assurance: The Legacy of Calvin and His Successors*, The Banner of Truth Trust, Edinburgh, 1999. Among Owen's works, see above all his *A Practical Exposition upon Psalm 130...*, in *The Works of John Owen*, The Banner of Truth Trust, London, 1966, Vol.6 pp321-648. In addition to Eaton's *Encouragement*, see his *No Condemnation: A Theology of Assurance of Salvation*, Piquant Editions, Carlisle, 2013.

subject, one which is of vital concern to many – even, for some, a matter of anguish: How can I, as a believer, be assured that I am, indeed, a true Christian? And how is this assurance connected with my sanctification?

I hope my book proves to be a help to anxious believers, brings unbelievers to Christ, and, in and through those ends, glorifies the triune God. After all, I can only write about the doctrine of assurance because God the Father decreed the salvation of his elect, God the Son accomplished it for them, and God the Spirit applies it to them.

Introduction

When Paul declared: 'The Son of God... loved me and gave himself for me' (Gal. 2:20), he was speaking with resounding confidence, telling us that he had a solid assurance that he was Christ's, and that Christ was his. The question is, of course, was he speaking as an apostle, as one specially favoured to be able to make such a declaration, or was he speaking as a typical believer? Can we, as believers, be as sure as Paul? Or was he simply telling the Galatians a wonderful fact about himself, but one which they could hardly hope to share, even after years of struggle?

Such scriptural examples and consequent questions could be multiplied. Is it only Paul, and a select few with him, who can say: 'In [Christ] and through faith in him we may approach God with freedom and confidence' (Eph. 3:12)? Is it only the select few who can declare: 'I know whom I have believed, and am convinced that he is able to guard what I have entrusted to him for that day' (2 Tim. 1:12)? Of whom, and to whom, was John speaking when he said: 'We know and rely on the love God has for us... We will have confidence on the day of judgement... There is no fear in love. But perfect love drives out fear, because fear has to do with punishment' (1 John 4:15-18)? Of whom was Paul speaking when he declared: 'God did not give us a spirit of timidity, but a spirit of power, of love and of self-discipline' (2 Tim. 1:7)? And when he told the Romans: 'You did not receive a spirit that makes you a slave again to fear, but you received the Spirit of sonship' (Rom. 8:15), were the Romans special – or did the apostle's words apply to all believers in his day? Indeed, do they apply to all believers today? Or do these words apply to a spiritual elite only: 'Now it is God who makes both us and you stand firm in Christ. He anointed us, set his seal of ownership on us, and put his Spirit in our hearts as a deposit, guaranteeing what is to come' (2 Cor. 1:21-22)? And so on.

Can there be any doubt? These words, all of them, were applicable to all believers at the time they were written, they remained so for all believers in all succeeding generations, and they are still applicable to all believers today. Or should be.

Reader, let me ask you another question: What is your basic overall view of Romans 7:14-25? I am not asking for detailed exposition of every word, you understand; just your overall view of the passage. Let me put it like this: Do you look upon Romans 7:14-25 as the description of the spiritual man at his most spiritual? Let me remind you of the words in question:

We know that the law is spiritual; but I am unspiritual, sold as a slave to sin. I do not understand what I do. For what I want to do I do not do, but what I hate I do. And if I do what I do not want to do, I agree that the law is good. As it is, it is no longer I myself who do it, but it is sin living in me. I know that nothing good lives in me, that is, in my flesh. For I have the desire to do what is good, but I cannot carry it out. For what I do is not the good I want to do; no, the evil I do not want to do – this I keep on doing. Now if I do what I do not want to do, it is no longer I who do it, but it is sin living in me that does it. So I find this law at work: When I want to do good, evil is right there with me. For in my inner being I delight in God's law; but I see another law at work in the members of my body, waging war against the law of my mind and making me a prisoner of the law of sin at work within my members. What a wretched man I am! Who will rescue me from this body of death?... So then, I myself in my mind am a slave to God's law, but in the flesh a slave to the law of sin (Rom. 7:14-25).[1]

Is the wretchedness, the defeat, the utter confusion, here spelled out by the apostle, typical of the believer? Is it representative of the Christian experience, the believer at his best?

Speaking for myself, I am not at all sure 'the man of Romans 7' exists. I am persuaded that above all the apostle is talking about the inadequacy of the law – the law's utter weakness, utter powerlessness and uselessness to save the sinner (Acts 13:39; Rom. 3:20; 8:3; Gal. 2:16; 3:21; Heb. 7:19; 9:9; 10:1); that is, its total inadequacy to justify, sanctify, liberate and glorify. In particular, in Romans 7, Paul is concerned to show the absolute incapability of the law when it comes to justification and sanctification. *That* is what Paul is teaching here. Of *that* there is not the slightest doubt. The context is invincible. And by 'the context', I mean Romans

---

[1] I have omitted: 'Thanks be to God – through Jesus Christ our Lord!' in order not to lose the sense of wretchedness and defeat which the apostle so clearly intends to delineate. The omitted words really belong to Romans before and after this particular section.

5:12 – 8:39; then the whole of Romans; then the whole of the New Testament dealing with events and people after Pentecost. Quite a context! Answering my own question, therefore, I am convinced that Romans 7:14-25 does *not* represent the believer at his best.

Putting all this together, it is clear that the New Testament speaks of believers as assured, confident of their position in Christ, full of joy – even in the most dire of circumstances, suffering and persecution – and very far from being wretched, doubting and lacking assurance.

As Alan Stibbs and James Packer noted:

James Denny once observed that the touchstone of any version of Christianity is its doctrine of assurance, and he illustrated his meaning by saying that, whereas in conventional Catholicism assurance is a sin, and in conventional Protestantism it is a duty, in the New Testament assurance is simply a fact. He was right. The New Testament never discusses assurance as a topic, because lack of assurance was not in those days a problem... Throughout the New Testament it is taken for granted that Christians are joyfully certain of their standing in God's grace, their sonship in his family, and their hope of his glory – all the good things, in fact, which are spelled out in sequence as belonging to 'us' – Paul and all his Christian readers – in chapter 8 of the letter to the Romans.[2]

Very well. New Testament believers were assured. That, surely, is a given. And this should be the lot of all true believers today. As D.Martyn Lloyd-Jones put it:

All Christian people are meant to have assurance of salvation... God has not only provided a way whereby we can be saved,[3] and not only saved us, but he has let us know that he has done so. This is a glorious aspect of the Christian life. The Christian is not meant to remain in doubt and uncertainty... In addition, the Christian is meant to know peace and joy.[4]

But many, today, are not assured – or, at least, they are struggling with the question.[5] John Newton: 'What is *now* thought *so*

---

[2] Stibbs and Packer p87.
[3] For my reservations on 'provide', see my *Particular*.
[4] Lloyd-Jones: *Warfare* pp221-222.
[5] In fact, although I have just quoted Lloyd-Jones with approval, it is ironic that he himself preached and wrote in a way that discouraged believers,

uncommon, in early days was spoken of as *the common portion of Christians*.[6] And he was referring to assurance.

And that is what I am concerned with here. I am trying to help believers who are in trouble over their assurance. I am convinced that in this matter, a gulf exists between the experience of most believers today and that of the believers in the New Testament. And I see one over-arching reason for this: we have moved away from the new covenant, and in two respects. Hence my title: *Assurance in The New Covenant*.

First, Sandemanianism is having a debilitating – not to say, devastating – effect in the lives of many professing believers. I will say little about this here since I intend to publish on it, but Sandemanianism is one of the great curses of our day.[7] In essence, it is an emphasis on the mind at the expense of the heart; an emphasis on doctrine, rather than felt experience; an emphasis on word, rather than Spirit. Do not miss my use of 'emphasis'. We must have mind and heart, doctrine and experience, word and Spirit, but where Sandemanianism gets a hold, mind, doctrine and word predominate at the expense of heart, experience and the Spirit. Today's Sandemanianism takes one of two forms – overt and incipient.

As for overt Sandemanianism, consider this:

Saving faith... A person either believes the offer of eternal life or he doesn't... If someone does believe the offer of eternal life – as the Bible presents this offer – he will also be sure that he has eternal life. This is what we mean when we say that assurance is of the essence of saving faith[8]... Let me just restate the matter in order to make it clear.

---

and actually manufactured difficulties for them in this matter of assurance – as I will prove.

[6] Pratt p221, emphasis his.

[7] A Sandemanian thinks saving faith is nothing more than mental assent. If a sinner accepts the facts of the gospel, he is saved. To talk about the heart, or feelings, is to introduce works, and ruin the grace of God in salvation. Sandemanianism was developed by the Scotsmen, John Glas (1695-1773) and his son-in-law, Robert Sandeman (1718-1771), more especially the latter. It is not a mere historical aberration. Rather, it is, forgiving the oxymoron, very much alive, and wreaking massive damage.

[8] 'The essence of faith' plays a big part in this debate. Although Hodges and Calvin are poles apart on the nature of faith, they are one in

The nature of the gospel message is such that, when a person believes it, he necessarily has assurance of eternal salvation. No matter what else he might believe, if he is not assured, he has not believed the gospel.

And what, in this system, is saving faith? Nothing more than mental assent:

To believe in Jesus is shorthand for to believe that Jesus is the Christ... There is no difference in kind between believing that Elvis [Presley] is alive and believing that Jesus is the Christ. Both are acts of faith. Of course, the former faith is unfounded. The latter is divinely sanctioned. The former is misplaced faith. The latter is saving faith.[9]

Sandemanianism, pure and simple! Utterly and fatally wrong! And such teaching leads to a wrong view of salvation (and, quite possibly, even to not being saved), false assurance and carnality, a toxic combination indeed!

Just one further example. This is how N.T.Wright described conversion: 'Understand... how to learn your lines and join in the drama'. This is a highly significant statement. 'Conversion', in Wright's scheme, has been replaced by becoming 'an actor in the play' and 'learning your lines'.[10] Coming (much) closer to home, there is a great deal of 'coaching' sinners into 'faith' these days. Those who run introductory courses (and I am thinking of other courses, far better courses, than Alpha – but not excluding it) and Bible studies for unbelievers ought, at the very least, to be aware of the exceedingly serious consequences of spoon-feeding them so that they can 'learn their lines', and so be counted converts. So much for overt Sandemanianism.

Incipient Sandemanianism – that is, Sandemanianism which is unrecognised, low-level, and part of 'the hidden curriculum'[11] – is

---

(mistakenly) believing that assurance is the essence of faith. See Appendix 1.

[9] Hodges. See Sawyer.

[10] Wright. Wright went further. Babies join in the play by being sprinkled.

[11] When I was a schoolmaster, I taught according to two curriculums. In the first, I taught Pythagoras' Theorem, Quadratic Equations, Integration by Parts, and so on. 'The hidden curriculum' was what I taught by my attitude and actions. For instance, I might say that homework is essential –

17

very common today, showing itself in a barren, 'intellectual', dry, detached, 'tick the boxes' experience – for the individual and the church. Let me be explicit. I am talking about lecturing instead of preaching, the delivering of boring addresses directed to the mind (if that!) at the expense of the heart and will, merely dealing out facts, describing the gospel, preaching sanctification by rule and recipe, and so on; this will produce incipient Sandemanians. The Bible shows us that the truth has to enter the mind, penetrate the heart, and govern the experience (Rom. 6:17; 10:8-13). The truth must warm and move. Incipient Sandemanianism fails miserably in this respect. And when this is combined, as it often is, with legal preaching instead of gospel preaching, one of the main casualties is the believer's assurance.[12] That is why, I remind you, I have called my book: *Assurance in The New Covenant*.

As I say, I hope to publish on all this, our first departure from the new covenant, and which has done so much damage to the doctrine and experience of assurance. But it is the second aspect of our move away from the new covenant – legal preaching – which I have in my sights at this time.

Under this legal system, we are told that we must preach the law to sinners to prepare them for Christ, bringing them to a sufficient sense of their sin to make them fit for trusting Christ,[13] and, once they are converted, take them back to the law for sanctification. Believers, so we are told, are lazy asses, and must be whipped by the law, driven by the law, to sanctification.[14] Then, we are told, for his assurance the believer must look to his sanctification – which he gets under the law. Hence I have (as far as I know) coined the expression 'legal assurance'.

In my preaching and my books, I have argued that legal preaching is wrong, both for the unbeliever and believer. In particular, for his sanctification and his assurance, the believer must not look to himself, must not look to his feelings, must not look to

---

but if I never marked a book, my pupils would grasp 'the hidden curriculum': homework doesn't matter!

[12] See Lloyd-Jones: *Warfare* p225.

[13] This is known as preparationism.

[14] For full documentation, see my *Christ*.

his works, must not look to the law, but must look to Christ; he must look to Christ for all.

But how does this square with John's first letter? Didn't the apostle set out a series of tests for the believer, tests which involve the believer in self-examination, making him look at his sanctification, and all in order to gain assurance? And what about passages such as: 'Examine yourselves to see whether you are in the faith; test yourselves. Do you not realise that Christ Jesus is in you – unless, of course, you fail the test?' (2 Cor. 13:5)? Or: 'A man ought to examine himself' (1 Cor. 11:28)? Don't these passages tell a believer to look to himself and his works, and do so for his assurance? And what about Peter's command: 'My brothers, be all the more eager to make your calling and election sure' (2 Pet. 1:10)?[15] How can my teaching survive when confronted by such Scriptures?

I want to address this question, but not merely to justify what I have preached and written. I want to do that, of course. I *must* do that. Even so, I have bigger fish, far more important fish, to fry. Just as, when I was preaching on passages of Scripture to do with the law, the believer, sanctification and assurance, and publishing books on the same, I hoped to glorify God in the edification of his people and the conversion of sinners, so here. In particular, I am still aiming to help those many believers who are in bondage over their sanctification and assurance, in bondage because they are being reared on a diet of law (in some form or another) and fear; in bondage because they are tied to a grinding treadmill of rule and regulation and consequent introspection. As far as I can judge by the literature, a high percentage of believers must be plodding on, gritting their teeth, burdened with fears and doubts, poring over their lack of sanctification, hoping against hope that on their death-

---

[15] And what about the warning passages (Heb. 6:4-20; 10:26 – 11:1; 12:14-29)? I take these warnings as real, and apply them to sanctification as an essential mark of conversion (Heb. 6:11-12; 10:14). Eaton thought they refer to rewards (Eaton: *Encouragement* pp214-217). 1 Cor. 3:12-15; 4:5 would bear this out. The writer to the Hebrews included immediate assurances for his readers concerning their salvation (Heb. 6:9; 10:39; 12:22-24,28).

bed they might – just might – get full assurance.[16] According to some teachers, the height of the believer's spirituality is to be in doubt and, consequently, to be miserable and fearful. And when such doubting saints come across someone who claims he is assured, 'presumption!' can often spring to the lips or into the mind.[17]

Well, of course, presumption is a distinct possibility, but is lack of assurance the hallmark of true spirituality? I fail to see it in the New Testament. I am most decidedly of the same opinion as Stibbs and Packer:

God, unlike many men, is utterly straightforward, and wants people to know where they stand with him. He wants unbelievers to be quite clear that without Christ they are lost, and equally he intends believers to be out of doubt that in Christ they are both saved and safe.[18]

A.W.Tozer got very close to what I want to say:

One distinguishing mark of those first Christians was a supernatural radiance that shined out from within them. The sun had come up in their hearts, and its warmth and light made unnecessary any secondary sources of assurance. They had the inner witness. It is obvious that the average evangelical Christian today is without this radiance. Instead of

---

[16] 'Full assurance' needs care. The phrase gives the impression that some believers get *full* assurance but, perhaps, most believers have to put up with a *lesser* assurance. This is quite wrong. The 'full assurance' in certain versions of Col. 2:2; 4:12; Heb. 6:11; 10:22 means 'complete, to make full, having been made full ' – yes, 'assured', 'confident', *but not in the sense we are thinking about*; namely, personal assurance of being in a state of grace. The context in each case makes this clear. Take Col. 2:2, for instance. Believers must be fully confident in their understanding and knowledge of the mystery of God; namely, Christ. Take Heb. 6:11. Believers should always be diligent to make sure they persevere, and so guarantee their entrance into all that God has prepared for his people.
[17] A reader told me that, when she was converted as a teenager, she wrote to her former Sunday School superintendent to let him know the good news. The gentleman replied with 'a blistering letter' telling her 'she should not be concerned to know she had an interest in Christ, but whether or not he had an interest in her'!
[18] Stibbs and Packer p85.

the inner witness, we now substitute logical conclusions drawn from texts.[19]

If Tozer had included 'works' along with 'texts', he would have made my point precisely.

One final word before we begin. When tackling this subject, we must not start with our experience and try to make Scripture fit that. Rather, we must start with Scripture, discover what that teaches, and then apply what we have learnt from God's word to our lives. Far too many teachers – not excluding some of the greatest – wrongly take the first course. Little wonder that they get themselves, and their hearers and readers, into serious difficulties.

Now let me set about the work.

---

[19] Tozer p18.

New-Covenant Assurance

This could be a very short chapter indeed. It ought to be! What does the New Testament say about assurance? Not much! Surprising as it may seem, the New Testament simply does not have a highly developed doctrine of assurance, certainly nothing to compare with what is set out in the works produced by legal teachers; apparently in those early days there was no call for such detailed instruction. This silence needs to be taken fully into account. Why does the New Testament not have anything along the lines of those books I mentioned at the beginning – books with many closely-argued pages on assurance?[1] Why, especially, is there nothing in the sacred pages that comes anywhere near Beeke's title: *The **Quest** for Full Assurance*? Why does the New Testament not tell us of believers who are engaged in a 'long and arduous search' for assurance? Since nearly all the New Testament letters were written to combat some sort of misunderstanding or error, some malady, or bondage to some sort of false teaching, I can only deduce that the early believers would be utterly fazed if they came back and could read the literature on the life-long 'quest' for assurance; the problem had not figured in their experience. Let me add a little to an earlier extract from Stibbs and Packer:

James Denny once observed that the touchstone of any version of Christianity is its doctrine of assurance, and he illustrated his meaning by saying that, whereas in conventional Catholicism assurance is a sin, and in conventional Protestantism it is a duty, in the New Testament

---

[1] I realise the same may be said about, say, justification. But there's a difference between the need to write a treatise on justification in order to refute false teaching on the subject, and the need for complicated explanations of what was common knowledge and experience in New Testament times. Applying to the matter in hand, to defend assurance against attack is one thing, but we are talking about *establishing* it. The apostles did the latter, and did it very briefly. So why is my chapter as long as it is? Because the New Testament doctrine of assurance has largely been forgotten, side-lined or denied, and replaced by a very different experience. Baptism is a parallel. The titles of my *Infant Baptism Tested* and *Baptist Sacramentalism: A Warning to Baptists* speak for themselves.

assurance is simply a fact. He was right. The New Testament never discusses assurance as a topic, because lack of assurance was not in those days a problem... Throughout the New Testament it is taken for granted that Christians are joyfully certain of their standing in God's grace, their sonship in his family, and their hope of his glory – all the good things, in fact, which are spelled out in sequence as belonging to 'us' – Paul and all his Christian readers – in chapter 8 of the letter to the Romans.[2]

So where has our problem come from? Where have we lost our way? Surely, we cannot allow that, while New Testament believers were assured, assurance is beyond the reach of most of us today. Of course not! The problem must be of our own making. It is! It comes largely from (overtly or incipiently) preaching law (in some form or another) instead of gospel: preaching the law to sinners to prepare them for Christ, and then, once they are converted, preaching the law to them in order to get them sanctified. This emphasis on law, this primacy of the law, has made a direct contribution to the bondage, introspection and lack of assurance of believers today. How? Legal preachers do not stop at sanctification: they compound the problem by their teaching on assurance. Hence the need for them to write their tomes on the subject, trying to deal with the grief and misery they themselves have produced. I will return to this in the following chapter. My present task is to establish the New Testament position.

Even though the New Testament does not have anything like the weighty books I mentioned, it does speak of assurance, and does so dogmatically and unequivocally. What is more, I make bold to say that it speaks simply. I say that, because 'ordinary' believers – in those early days, some of whom were slaves and probably couldn't even read – were assured! Apparently, today, we need a PhD in theology, and another in church history, plus more than a smattering of philosophy, to enable us to understand what we are talking about, and then to nerve us to set out on the gruelling and drawn-out search for the peace, hope and rest that comes from the

---

[2] Stibbs and Packer p87. As I have said, I will look at passages which seem to command believers to probe themselves as to the reality of their faith. But even if we take these at face value, the idea of a life-long, often fruitless, quest for assurance is utterly foreign to the text.

assurance that we truly are the Lord's! But we aren't discussing how many angels we can cram onto the head of a pin. Doesn't every believer want to have assurance? Isn't assurance basic to the Christian life? How can believers have 'inexpressible and glorious joy' (1 Pet. 1:8) if they don't even know that they are believers? What books on the subject of assurance did Peter's readers need or have? Indeed, as I will show, if they had possessed such volumes as law teachers produce, they would have discovered that most of them would never get the joy they were seeking – or, rather, they would learn that they were either among the elite, or else they were presumptuous. The fact is, however, Peter's readers did not even seek joy: they had it! Assurance was not a grind, a duty, a struggle; in those early days, it was a fact of spiritual life!

What is the ground of the believer's assurance in the New Testament? This is the real issue. Let us bring our experience or theological system into the picture only after we have established scriptural teaching. What is the New Testament ground of assurance? Is it sanctification? That is, is a believer to gain assurance by testing himself as to his works and sanctification? Is *this* the way of assurance? It is usually regarded as such today. But, even though the majority of believers are taught that it is so – and, by believing it, are struggling with the consequences – this is not the New Testament way. As the apostles made perfectly clear, the way to assurance is not through the believer's sanctification, but by the witness of the Spirit.

In saying this, I don't want to be misunderstood. Just as the *unbeliever*, in his conversion, believes the promise of God – the promise drawn from 'the holy Scriptures, which are able to make [him] wise for salvation through faith in Christ Jesus' (2 Tim. 3:15) – so the *believer* bases his hope and assurance on Christ revealed and contained in that promise (John 6:35; Rom. 5:1; Heb. 4:3; 1 Pet. 1:8). This ought to be taken as read! Faith comes by hearing the word of God, the word concerning Christ (Rom. 10:17), and faith involves trust of that word leading to trust in Christ. So it is with assurance. The believer trusts God's promise to him: if he believes, he will be saved (Acts 16:31). As a consequence, he trusts Christ. But just as the *unbeliever* needs the power of the Spirit to enable him to repent and believe (John 6:44; Acts 5:31; Eph. 2:8-

10), so the *believer* needs – and is given – the power and grace to believe God's promise for assurance. God gives him the grace and power so to trust – and he does so trust the promise for assurance by the same Spirit who taught him to believe for salvation in the first place. The child of God is persuaded, not only that when he trusted Christ, God kept his word, and saved him, but that he will go on keeping his word, and will save him right to the end: 'I know whom I have believed, and am convinced that he is able to guard what I have entrusted to him for that day' (2 Tim. 1:12). That 'believing' comes, under the terms of the new covenant, from the Scriptures by the Spirit's inward instruction:

It is written in the prophets: 'They will all be taught by God'. Everyone who listens to the Father and learns from him comes to me (John 6:45). I will put my laws in their minds and write them on their hearts. I will be their God, and they will be my people. No longer will a man teach his neighbour, or a man his brother, saying: 'Know the Lord', because they will all know me, from the least of them to the greatest (Heb. 8:10-11; 10:16).

But this, marvellous as it is, far from exhausts the Spirit's work in the believer in this matter of assurance. He graciously does far more than enable the believer to rely on God's promise. At conversion, something far more wonderful occurs. Listen to Paul:

If anyone does not have the Spirit of Christ, he does not belong to Christ... Those who are led by the Spirit of God are sons of God. For you did not receive a spirit that makes you a slave again to fear, but you received the Spirit of sonship. And by him we cry: 'Abba, Father'. The Spirit himself testifies with our spirit that we are God's children. Now if we are children, then we are heirs – heirs of God and co-heirs with Christ, if indeed we share in his sufferings in order that we may also share in his glory... We... have the firstfruits of the Spirit (Rom. 8:9,14-17,23).
Now it is God who... anointed us, set his seal of ownership on us, and put his Spirit in our hearts as a deposit, guaranteeing what is to come (2 Cor. 1:21-22).
God... has given us the Spirit as a deposit, guaranteeing what is to come (2 Cor. 5:5).
Because you are sons, God sent the Spirit of his Son into our [your] hearts, the Spirit who calls out: 'Abba, Father'. So you are no longer a slave, but a son; and since you are a son, God has made you also an heir (Gal. 4:6-7).

You also were included in Christ when you heard the word of truth, the gospel of your salvation. Having believed, you were marked in him with a seal, the promised Holy Spirit, who is a deposit guaranteeing our inheritance until the redemption of those who are God's possession – to the praise of his glory... Do not grieve the Holy Spirit of God, with whom you were sealed for the day of redemption (Eph. 1:13-14; 4:30).

And then John:

You have an anointing from the Holy One, and all of you know the truth. I do not write to you because you do not know the truth, but because you do know it and because no lie comes from the truth... As for you, the anointing you received from him remains in you, and you do not need anyone to teach you. But as his anointing teaches you about all things and as that anointing is real, not counterfeit – just as it has taught you, remain in him (1 John 2:20-27).
This is how we know that he lives in us: we know it by the Spirit he gave us (1 John 3:24).
We know that we live in him and he in us, because he has given us of his Spirit (1 John 4:13).
It is the Spirit who testifies, because the Spirit is the truth... We accept man's testimony, but God's testimony is greater because it is the testimony of God, which he has given about his Son. Anyone who believes in the Son of God has this testimony in his heart. Anyone who does not believe God has made him out to be a liar, because he has not believed the testimony God has given about his Son. And this is the testimony: God has given us eternal life, and this life is in his Son (1 John 5:6,9-11).[3]

This is New Testament assurance. Here we meet the three great phrases which lie at the heart of that assurance: 'the witness of the Spirit', 'the sealing of the Spirit' and 'the anointing with the Spirit'. Although there has been a debate as to whether or not these three are one and the same, I take them to be so. If they aren't, what scriptures tell us how to distinguish them, and speak of believers who have one or the other, but not all? In any case, notice how the terms are used almost interchangeably within the extracts above.

Working on the basis, then, that these different phrases speak of one and the same thing – the witness, anointing or sealing of the

---

[3] In addition, we have the repeated experience of 'being filled with the Spirit' (Luke 1:15,41,67; 4:1; Acts 2:4; 4:8,31; 6:3,5; 9:17; 11:24; 13:52; Eph. 5:18).

Spirit – observe how the New Testament takes it absolutely for granted – *absolutely for granted, I say* – that every believer has been anointed and sealed with the Spirit, and has the witness of the Spirit. There is not the slightest whiff of a hint of a suggestion that this experience of the Spirit is something extraordinary, reserved for just a few special believers, who, perhaps, after years of desperate struggle and earnest longing for it, come into a second, further, more glorious experience beyond conversion.

Let us remind ourselves of the obvious! Take the Ephesian extracts. Paul wrote to the *believers* at Ephesus, opening his letter thus: 'Paul, an apostle of Christ Jesus by the will of God, to the saints in Ephesus, the faithful in Christ Jesus' (Eph. 1:1); that is, he was addressing believers. Further, all these believers, as he said, 'were included in Christ when [they] heard the word of truth, the gospel of [their] salvation' (Eph. 1:13). They were included in Christ *as* they believed. The apostle was not writing to the elders, to the experienced and aged saints on their death-bed. No! He was writing to the *believers* at Ephesus, all the believers. Moreover there is no reason to think that these Ephesian believers were any different to us. There was nothing exceptional about them. Some, no doubt, were strong believers, some were weak; some were old believers, some were young; some had been believers a long time, some were new converts. They were men and women just like us – if we are believers. That's the only thing we can say about them: they were all believers. No! That's *not* the only thing we can say about them: they were all believers, they were all included in Christ, *and they were all sealed with the Spirit; **all** of them were.*

Take the Corinthian passages. We know that Paul wrote to the *believers* at Corinth: 'To the church of God in Corinth, to those sanctified in Christ Jesus and called to be holy, together with all those everywhere who call on the name of our Lord Jesus Christ-- their Lord and ours' (1 Cor. 1:1:2). 'To the church of God in Corinth, together with all the saints throughout Achaia' (2 Cor. 1:1). Now we know that the Corinthian believers, as a church, as a body of believers, were in a dreadful condition,[4] spiritually speaking. And yet, even so, as believers, all of them had the seal of

---

[4] Party spirit, yielding to contemporary culture, incest, indiscipline, disorder, doctrinal misunderstanding, and so on.

the Spirit, marking them out as believers, guaranteeing them their eternal glory, and witnessing to them that they were indeed the children of God: 'Now it is God who... anointed us, set his seal of ownership on us, and put his Spirit in our hearts as a deposit, guaranteeing what is to come... God... has given us the Spirit as a deposit, guaranteeing what is to come' (2 Cor. 1:21-22; 5:5). Even though the apostle rebuked them over several issues, although they urgently needed to repent and reform themselves, nevertheless they were still believers, and as such they were all sealed with the Spirit, this being fundamental to the Christian experience.

Let me work this out by returning to Ephesians 1:13-14:

You also were included in Christ when you heard the word of truth, the gospel of your salvation. Having believed, you were marked in him with a seal, the promised Holy Spirit, who is a deposit guaranteeing our inheritance until the redemption of those who are God's possession – to the praise of his glory.

Paul is explicit. Every believer is sealed with the Spirit at the time of his conversion; as the sinner comes to Christ by faith, he is united to Christ and is given the witness of the Spirit. Before we go any further, let me quote the passage in the AV. I do so because it has been the source of a great deal of misunderstanding about this very important subject:

In whom ye also trusted, after that ye heard the word of truth, the gospel of your salvation: in whom also after that ye believed, ye were sealed with that holy Spirit of promise, which is the earnest of our inheritance until the redemption of the purchased possession, unto the praise of his glory.

It is the second 'after' in the above which is the point at issue: '*After* that ye believed, ye were sealed'. As far as I know, the AV stands alone – if not, then almost alone – in including the 'after'.[5] *And it is quite wrong.* The second 'after' was inserted by the AV translators, who were acting as interpreters and commentators at this point, not translators. Sadly, this totally unwarranted insertion has led many (mistakenly) to think there is a gap between believing

---

[5] Tyndale's Bible translation had: 'In whom also ye (after that ye heard the word of truth I mean the gospel of your salvation wherein ye believed) were sealed'.

and being sealed. There is no such suggestion in the Greek; none whatever. Indeed, Paul's very point is that it is as the sinner believes – when he believes, in his believing – that he is sealed by the Spirit. The hearing, the believing, the union to Christ and the sealing of the Spirit are all simultaneous. Let me give the literal rendering of the apostle's Greek:

In whom also you, having heard the word of truth, the glad tidings of your salvation – in whom also, having believed, you were sealed with the Spirit of promise the Holy, who is [the] earnest of our inheritance, to [the] redemption of the acquired possession, to [the] praise of his glory.

The point is, there is no thought of any time lag between believing, inclusion in Christ, and the sealing of the Spirit. Any notion of such a gap is an unwarranted intrusion into the text. As Gordon D.Fee, speaking of 'the believing' and 'the receiving of the Spirit', declared:

These are two sides of the same coin... There is simply nothing in the context, not anything in this bit of grammar, that would cause [or allow – DG] one to think that Paul intends to refer here to two distinct experiences.[6]

Herman Bavinck:

When those who are pre-ordained by God are called in time... then at that very moment they obtain faith and by that faith they receive justification and the adoption as children (Rom. 3:22,24; 4:5; 5:1; Gal. 3:26; 4:5; *etc.*), with the assurance of sonship by the witness of the Holy Spirit (Rom. 8:15-16; Gal. 4:6; 2 Cor. 1:22; Eph. 1:13; 4:30)... In that moment... God acquits believers in their conscience and by his Spirit bears witness with their own spirits that they are children of God and heirs of eternal life (*cf.* Rom. 8:15-17)... By that Spirit, they are continually led... assured of the love that God has for them (Rom. 5:5,8) and of their adoption (Rom. 8:15-16; Gal. 4:6), and are now already the beneficiaries of peace (Rom. 5:1; Phil. 4:7,9; 1 Thess. 5:23), joy (Rom. 14:17; 15:13; 1 Thess. 1:6), and eternal life (John 3:16)... In Christ... the law has attained its end (Rom. 10:4): believers are free from the law (Gal. 4:26 – 5:1)...[7] and have received this spirit

---

[6] Fee: *God's* p670.
[7] Bavinck wrongly limited this to 'the curse of the law'.

of adoption, the spirit of freedom (Rom. 8:15; 2 Cor. 3:16-17; Gal. 5:18).[8]

According to Ephesians 1:13-14, then, every believer, coming to faith, is included in Christ when he hears the word of truth; better, *as* he hears the word of truth. At that moment – the moment he believes and is included in Christ – he is marked with a seal, sealed with the Holy Spirit.

And this can only mean assurance.

Let me reinforce the point from Romans 8:14-16. Paul declares: 'Those who are led by the Spirit of God are sons of God. For you did not receive a spirit that makes you a slave again to fear, but you received the Spirit of sonship. And by him we cry: "Abba, Father". The Spirit himself testifies with our spirit that we are God's children'. In this apostolic statement, there is no break anywhere, no hint of one. *We must not insert any gap or pause.* In particular, we must not insert a gap between: 'And by him we cry: "Abba, Father"', and: 'The Spirit himself testifies with our spirit that we are God's children'. There is no break in the text, and there is no interlude in the believer's experience. It is all one episode, one encounter with God through Christ by the Spirit. We are talking about conversion. In his conversion (which is brought about by the Spirit), the believer has his fear removed, is given a sense of sonship, is enabled to call God his Father, and is given the witness of the Spirit. Indeed, it is all one, all of a piece. There is no suggestion that the believer has his fear removed, is given the spirit of sonship and enabled to call God his Father, but is *not*, at the same time, given the witness of the Spirit – indeed, that he has embark on what will almost certainly turn out to be a fruitless quest for it! The Spirit grants all four experiences to the believer at the point of conversion. In truth, they form one experience.[9]

Let me summarise the ground we have covered. Assurance comes by trusting God's promise, yes, but supremely it comes by the direct witness of the Spirit to the believer's spirit: the Spirit seals

---

[8] Bavinck pp50,219,227,451.

[9] Not only so, the experience is not only a one-off; it is continuous, as I will show.

the believer, anoints him, and bears witness to him that he is indeed a child of God, an adopted son of God.

There's a missing note. Did you spot it? Sanctification! I have been paraphrasing Scripture – nothing else – and from trust in Christ to assurance there is no mention of 'sanctification'. Now that is remarkable! Why? Because sanctification is *the* way of assurance today – or so a good many teachers tell us. According to them, it is the sovereign way. As you can see, reader, this must be wrong. Sanctification is not the main way of assurance.

Let me prove it. Since, according to the New Testament, assurance comes immediately upon conversion by the anointing of the Spirit, sanctification (which is a life-long progressive growth) cannot possibly be the fundamental ground and way of assurance. The newest convert has the Spirit,[10] has the witness of the Spirit, is sealed by the Spirit, is anointed by the Spirit, is led by the Spirit, has been adopted as a son and been given the spirit of sonship, and is given the Spirit to confirm all this to his spirit, granting him the confidence, at once, to call God his Father, Abba – possibly, even Daddy (or its equivalent) – (Rom. 8:14-17; 2 Cor. 1:21-22; Gal. 4:5-7; Eph. 1:13-14; 4:30; 1 John 2:20-27; 4:13; 5:6,9-11). *But he has only just begun to live a life of sanctification. Yet that believer has the joy of assurance, must have that assurance to be able to call God his Father.* The believer's assurance, in the first instance, therefore, must arise from the witness of the Spirit, and not from his sanctification – as law teachers maintain. The witness of the Spirit must be fundamental to assurance, and assurance by the witness of the Spirit must precede any assurance by evidences of sanctification. Thus the apostle could demand of the Galatians: 'Are you so foolish? Having begun in the Spirit, are you now being made perfect by the flesh?... He who supplies the Spirit to you... does he do it by the works of the law, or by the hearing of faith?' (Gal. 3:3-5, NKJV). The Galatians, having listened to law teachers, had suffered loss: 'What has happened to all your joy?' demanded the apostle (Gal. 4:15). These words, as a health warning to potential readers, need to be written large over all the tomes which

---

[10] He couldn't be regenerate without the Spirit. And, of course, we have: 'If anyone does not have the Spirit of Christ, he does not belong to Christ' (Rom. 8:9).

teach legal-assurance-by-sanctification. Assurance is by the witness of the Spirit, which witness starts[11] the moment the sinner believes.

I give two scriptural examples to support my case: the eunuch and the jailer. The eunuch was converted under Philip's teaching and was baptised by him: 'Both Philip and the eunuch went down into the water and Philip baptised him. When they came up out of the water, the Spirit of the Lord suddenly took Philip away, and the eunuch did not see him again, but went on his way rejoicing' (Acts 8:38-39). The jailer, converted under the ministry of Paul and Silas, 'was filled with joy because he had come to believe in God' (Acts 16:34). I admit that Luke does not say that the eunuch and the jailer were assured, but what else can his words mean?[12] Both men had 'joy'. In the eunuch's case, Luke used a word based on *kairō*, 'to rejoice, to be glad'; in the jailer's case, *agalliaō*, 'to exult with extreme joy, to rejoice exceedingly'.[13] I cannot see how these two men were anything but assured, yet in neither case could their assurance have come from their sanctification. Their joy preceded their sanctification which could hardly be said to have begun. Their assurance could have come only from the witness of the Spirit.

Now what is this witness of the Spirit? To whom does he witness? And to what does he witness?

In order to answer that, we need to go back to the beginning, starting with the unbeliever and the Spirit's work in conversion. No, this is not a digression!

The Spirit's work in the unbeliever leading to conversion
Conversion. What does the Bible mean by it? We must not take this for granted. Since, as I will show, poor – not to say, false – teaching can and does damage believers over this matter of assurance, we must be clear what we are talking about when we speak of conversion. The truth is, inadequate handling of the souls of men *at the point of conversion* leads to serious residual trouble for the

---

[11] I will return to this idea of 'starts'.

[12] In any case, there's no record of either man – or any other convert in those days – being told to set out on a life-long struggle for assurance, being given a detailed route-map for the journey, and yet warned that the quest will, in all probability, be fruitless.

[13] Thayer.

believer. Going wrong here is akin to the kind of serious damage that can be caused by defective care at a natural birth.

Consider Ephesians 1:13-14 once again. What can we learn about conversion from these two verses?

You also were included in Christ when you heard the word of truth, the gospel of your salvation. Having believed, you were marked in him with a seal, the promised Holy Spirit, who is a deposit guaranteeing our inheritance until the redemption of those who are God's possession – to the praise of his glory.

First of all, we have to hear the word of truth, the gospel of salvation. Let me underline this. It has to be the gospel that we hear, and we have to hear it. It must, therefore, be the *gospel* – not law – that has to be preached.[14] How little gospel preaching there is today! Not only do we too often hear something other than the gospel, too often we are fed on lectures and not preaching. We have historical lectures, lectures on doctrine, lectures on theology, lectures on creeds, lectures on Confessions, lectures on personal relationships and self-fulfilment, lectures on social matters... and I don't know what else! We must follow the apostle and preach the gospel. And what is it to preach the gospel? It is to preach Christ:

I resolved to know nothing... except Jesus Christ and him crucified (1 Cor. 2:2).
When I preach the gospel, I cannot boast, for I am compelled to preach. Woe to me if I do not preach the gospel! (1 Cor. 9:16).
By setting forth the truth plainly... our gospel.. the light of the gospel of the glory of Christ... We... preach... Jesus Christ as Lord (2 Cor. 4:2-5).

This – the preaching of the gospel – is what converted sinners at Ephesus, Corinth and Rome. It wasn't preaching the law! It wasn't a talk on personal relationships, it wasn't a talk on self-fulfilment, it wasn't a historical lecture. It was the preaching of Christ to them as sinners. That was what brought them to Christ. If we do not preach

---

[14] When I say 'preached', it could be standing in a pulpit, but it could be in a multitude of other ways: a mother talking to a child on her lap or by her knee, a father witnessing to his son, a neighbour talking to a friend, a college student talking to a fellow-student, a conversation at the bus stop, in a supermarket, and so on.

the gospel, and preach out properly, we can damage believers as they come to faith, *and that damage can afflict them for the rest of their pilgrimage*. This fact alone is sufficient to show that we must avoid the common misconception that teaching for the saints is difficult, but preaching to sinners is a doddle. Not only do I abhor the notion that we should not preach the gospel to saints – we should always preach the gospel (Acts 20:20-21,24-27; Rom. 1:1; 1 Cor. 1:17; 2:2; 9:16; 2 Cor. 4:5; Gal. 1:1, and so on) – bringing sinners to Christ needs sensitive care. Much damage can be caused by poor handling at this most sensitive point.

Returning to Ephesians: Paul went on: 'You heard the word of truth'. You *heard* it. What does that mean? Does it mean we have to hear with the ear? Well, that's the first thing we have to do – we have to hear it. Yet even here we need to be clear. A man might be deaf, and yet he can still hear the gospel preached. Is that possible? Yes! He can read the text. In some way or another the word can reach him. The word must reach the sinner.

But that's just the start. When Paul said 'hear', he was going much further than physical hearing. The sound must go deeper than the ear. I'm afraid that many, when they listen to preaching, hear it only physically. Their minds are miles away: they're thinking about the golf match, the bowling tournament, their holiday, what they can have for lunch, what they're doing tomorrow, what's on the television, or whatever. The truth has reached the ear, and that's all. When Paul says: 'You heard the word of truth', he means that it penetrated their ear and got into their mind.

Yet even this is not enough. I'm afraid that many stop there. They think that it's enough for the truth to reach the mind, and that's all there is to it. *But this is not saving.* A man may assent to the truth, and not be saved. The truth must reach the heart, the will, the emotions, the very centre of the man. The truth must reach the soul.

And it must be appropriated. The sinner has to believe, to trust Christ. Saving trust in Christ is essential.[15] As Paul put it: 'The Son of God, who loved me and gave himself for me' (Gal. 2:20). 'I have heard the truth', he says. 'I knew it was right. But, above all, I

---

[15] More is involved: conviction, repentance and so on, but Eph. 1:13-14 concentrates on 'faith'.

believed, I knew, I felt, it was for me. I trusted Christ. And now I know that Christ is mine'. The sinner has to hear about Christ, and believe the gospel record, yes, but saving faith is more than 'believing the record'. The sinner has to call upon Christ, to trust Christ: 'believing', 'hearing', 'receiving', 'welcoming', 'trusting' Christ – it's all the same. And 'trust' lies at the heart of conversion.

Now, at the very moment the sinner believes, in the act of believing, something remarkable takes place: he is included in Christ (Eph. 1:13). What is this being 'in Christ', a phrase written large across the New Testament? The GNB translates the phrase excellently as 'union with Christ'. 'In Christ' is union with Christ. This is the great theme of the new Testament. Believers are in Christ, united to Christ.

What does that mean? It means that as God views his Son, so he views the believer. Just let that sink in! As God sees his Son, he sees the believer. But Christ is perfect! That's how God sees the believer! There is no condemnation to any man who is in Christ Jesus (Rom. 8:1). He has passed from death to life (1 John 3:14). He is out of Adam and in Christ (Rom. 5:12-21; 1 Cor. 15:22,45). He has been transferred out of Satan's realm into the kingdom of Christ (Col. 1:13). As Christ is to the Father – loved, perfect, sinless – so is the believer: he is without spot or wrinkle or stain or any such thing in his sight (Eph. 5:27; Heb. 10:14). The believer is completely free of sin before God. All the sinner's sin has been laid on Christ (Isa. 53:6; Gal. 3:13), and all Christ's righteousness has been accounted to the believer (Rom. 3:22; 1 Cor. 1:30; 2 Cor. 5:21). This is what Paul means by telling believers they are 'included in Christ'. Other passages speak of Christ being in the believer. Just so! The believer is united to Christ, one with Christ. And having begun a good work in the believer, God will go on perfecting it, even to the day of Christ Jesus (Phil. 1:6). This is the gospel. And the gospel has to be taught and preached in order to bring sinners to Christ. As Paul told the Corinthians:

Christ... [sent] me... to preach the gospel... For the message of the cross is foolishness to those who are perishing, but to us who are being saved it is the power of God... God [is] pleased through the foolishness of what was preached to save those who believe (1 Cor. 1:17-18,21).

What role does the Spirit play in all this? An absolutely vital role! Paul made this the acid test: 'If anyone does not have the Spirit of Christ, he does not belong to Christ' (Rom. 8:9). He explained: 'No one who is speaking by the Spirit of God says: "Jesus be cursed", and no one can say: "Jesus is Lord", except by the Holy Spirit' (1 Cor. 12:3). The gift and work of the Spirit are essential.

But all is well: Christ promised to give his Spirit for this very work: 'I will pour out my Spirit', he said, Peter declaring the same on the day of Pentecost (see Acts 2:17-18). As the apostle went on to tell his enquirers during that same discourse:

Repent and be baptised, every one of you, in the name of Jesus Christ for the forgiveness of your sins. And you will receive the gift of the Holy Spirit. The promise is for you and your children and for all who are far off – for all whom the Lord our God will call (Acts 2:38-39).[16]

Christ's promised Holy Spirit comes to the sinner in order to regenerate him – that's how the sinner believes. No sinner can believe until the Spirit gives him life and the will to believe (John 6:44-45). The sinner, being dead, will never come to me, said Christ, and all men are dead in sins by nature (Eph. 2:1-3). Sinners have to be regenerated, born again before they can believe. The dead can't believe, the deaf can't hear, and the blind can't see, but Christ can do the impossible! As he physically raised the dead man, made the blind man see, opened the ears of the deaf, and enabled the man to stretch out his withered arm, so spiritually: by his Spirit, Christ makes the spiritually dead live, the spiritually blind see, the spiritually deaf hear, the spiritually lame leap (Isa. 35:5-6). He regenerates them by his Spirit. As Jesus told Nicodemus:

I tell you the truth, no one can see the kingdom of God unless he is born again... I tell you the truth, no one can enter the kingdom of God unless he is born of water and the Spirit. Flesh gives birth to flesh, but the Spirit gives birth to spirit. You should not be surprised at my saying: 'You must be born again'. The wind blows wherever it pleases. You hear its sound, but you cannot tell where it comes from or where it is going. So it is with everyone born of the Spirit (John 3:3-8).

As Paul reminded Titus, speaking of all believers:

---

[16] That there is more in this promise than I speak of here, I freely admit. See my *Baptist*.

[God] saved us through the washing of rebirth and renewal by the Holy Spirit, whom he poured out on us generously through Jesus Christ our Saviour (Tit. 3:5-6).

That's just the start. In regenerating the sinner, the Spirit works yet more grace in him; he convicts him of his sin, and the glories of Christ and his work:

When he comes, he will convict the world of guilt in regard to sin and righteousness and judgement: in regard to sin, because men do not believe in me; in regard to righteousness, because I am going to the Father, where you can see me no longer; and in regard to judgement, because the prince of this world now stands condemned (John 16:8-11).

Christ, having regenerated the sinner, and convicted him of his sin by his Spirit, gives him the grace to believe:

For it is by grace you have been saved, through faith – and this not from yourselves, it is the gift of God – not by works, so that no one can boast (Eph. 2:8-9).[17]

Thus the Spirit comes to the unregenerate sinner, regenerates, convicts him, and brings him to Christ, to trust in Christ.

This, then, is the Spirit's work in conversion. In thinking of the believer's assurance, this work of the Spirit in the unbeliever must not be skipped. No sinner can have biblical comfort and assurance until he has first been regenerated, come under conviction of sin, and been converted to Christ: conviction of sin before conversion, and conversion before comfort.

All this would seem self-evident. But today it is not! As I have shown, contemporary Sandemanians are in danger – to put it no stronger – of claiming assurance without conviction and conversion. *Mental assent to certain facts (even gospel facts) is not saving.* So I say again: conviction of sin before conversion, and conversion before comfort. I go further. The Spirit who convicts and converts the unbeliever, is the same Spirit who assures the believer: *conviction and conversion by the Spirit will lead to comfort by the Spirit.*

---

[17] Christ gives grace to believe *and to repent* (Acts 5:31). Repentance is essential (Luke 24:47; Acts 2:38).

So much for the unbeliever.

The work of the Spirit in the believer leading to assurance
The Spirit's work does not stop with regeneration, conviction, faith
and conversion. As the sinner believes, something else happens to
him. *And this is the material point.* As he believes, the believer is
joined to Christ, included in Christ: 'You also were included in
Christ... having believed' (Eph. 1:13). As I have explained, through
his union with Christ, the believer stands as Christ in the sight of
God. All that Christ is, all that Christ has done, all that Christ has,
is made over and accounted to the believer. And this transaction, of
course, is carried out by the Spirit.

But even this does not exhaust the Spirit's work in the believer
at conversion. As the sinner believes, he is not only included in
Christ, but he is marked in Christ, sealed in Christ, sealed with the
Spirit, anointed by the Spirit, the Spirit bearing witness to him and
with him that he is indeed a child of God. In fact, the Spirit himself
is the seal, the guarantee, the deposit and foretaste of the eternal
glory which is eternally prepared for him as a child of God. The
believer, therefore, having the Spirit, must have the work of the
Spirit, *including the witness of the Spirit*, within himself: if any man
is not regenerate, does not trust Christ, does not have the seal, does
not have the Spirit of Christ, he doesn't belong to him (Rom. 8:9).

But, of course, the believer has it all, because he has Christ
through the Spirit. Finally, all this is in Christ. In himself, the
believer is a sinner, but in Christ he is perfect in the sight of God,
and marked as a child of God, and has the witness of the Spirit
bearing witness with his spirit that he is indeed in Christ, a child of
God. Christ has taken away his sin, and the Spirit takes away his
fear: the sinner is free from sin, law, death and fear – and the Spirit
tells him so.

Let me trace this out a little more fully. The question is: how
does the Spirit assure the believer? Jesus told us what the Spirit
would do in and to the believer. I say 'would do'; now it is 'will
do', even 'does'! Every believer has the Spirit (John 7:39; 14:17;
Acts 10:47; Rom. 8:9-17; 1 Cor. 2:12; 3:16; 6:19; 2 Cor. 1:22; 5:5;
Gal. 3:2,14; 4:4-7; 5:5,16-26; 6:8; Eph. 1:13-14,17; 2:22; 4:30; 1
Thess. 4:8; 1 John 2:20,27; 4:13; 5:6-11), but this cannot be in

order to regenerate him, since he is a believer already, and so must be regenerate.

So what does the Spirit do in every believer? Christ made it clear that it is the Father's will that all men (believers now – and all men in the day of judgement – Philippians 2:10-11) must glorify Christ, that they should 'honour the Son just as they honour the Father' (John 5:23). And it is precisely at this point that the Spirit works in the believer, bearing witness in and to him. Paul could say: 'The Son of God... loved me and gave himself for me' (Gal. 2:20). Where did he get such assurance? Can there be any doubt? The Spirit bore witness with his spirit, giving him his sense of sonship and adoption.

Christ promised the Spirit to every believer:

'Whoever believes in me, as the Scripture has said, streams of living water will flow from within him'. By this he meant the Spirit, whom those who believed in him were later to receive. Up to that time the Spirit had not been given, since Jesus had not yet been glorified (John 7:38-39).

As Christ went on to say:

I will ask the Father, and he will give you another Counsellor to be with you forever – the Spirit of truth. The world cannot accept him, because it neither sees him nor knows him. But you know him, for he lives with you and will be in you... the Counsellor, the Holy Spirit, whom the Father will send in my name, will teach you all things and will remind you of everything I have said to you (John 14:16-17,26).

And Christ was explicit as to the Spirit's mission with regard to the believer:

When the Counsellor comes, whom I will send to you from the Father, the Spirit of truth who goes out from the Father, he will testify about me... When he, the Spirit of truth, comes, he will guide you into all truth. He will not speak on his own; he will speak only what he hears, and he will tell you what is yet to come. He will bring glory to me by taking from what is mine and making it known to you. All that belongs to the Father is mine. That is why I said the Spirit will take from what is mine and make it known to you (John 15:26; 16:13-15).

And the Spirit's witness with our spirit that we are one of God's children is a vital part of this.[18] Let me re-quote the relevant scriptures:

Those who are led by the Spirit of God are sons of God. For you did not receive a spirit that makes you a slave again to fear, but you received the Spirit of sonship. And by him we cry: 'Abba, Father'. The Spirit himself testifies with our spirit that we are God's children. Now if we are children, then we are heirs – heirs of God and co-heirs with Christ (Rom. 8:14-17).

Because you are sons, God sent the Spirit of his Son into our [your] hearts, the Spirit who calls out: 'Abba, Father'. So you are no longer a slave, but a son; and since you are a son, God has made you also an heir (Gal. 4:6-7).

How does the Spirit do this? How does he bear witness to us? What did Paul mean when, on another issue, he said: 'My conscience confirms it in the Holy Spirit', 'my conscience bearing me witness in the Holy Spirit' (NASB) (Rom. 9:4)? According to Gill, Paul was saying:

Either that his conscience was influenced and directed by the Holy Ghost in what he was about to say, or [that] it bore witness in and with the Holy Ghost, and the Holy Ghost with [it]. So that here are three witnesses called in: Christ, conscience, and the Holy Ghost. And by three such witnesses, his words must be thought to be well established.

I ask again: How does the Spirit bear witness to us and with us? The answer takes us to the very heart of the new covenant. Let me

---

[18] Modern-day Sandemanians, taking faith as assent, argue that the Spirit does not witness *to the believer*, but joins the believer in witnessing *to God* that the believer is indeed a son of God: 'The Holy Spirit bears witness along with our human spirit that we are children of God. But to whom does he bear witness?... Our witness is to God the Father. If the Spirit is bearing witness *with* our human spirits, then he, too, must bear witness to God the Father... God the Father is the one to whom our human spirits, and the Holy Spirit, bear witness' (Wilkin, emphasis his). Why the Father 'needs' this witness, I fail to see. *The believer* needs it! Sandemanians give the impression, at least, that they are determined to avoid any suggestion of heart-feeling, warmth or delight in the believer. What an arid experience! Sadly, because of incipient Sandemanianism, too often 'arid experience' seems to be the norm! Coupled with an emphasis upon law (again, often incipient) things could hardly be worse.

begin at the beginning – with the original, great promise of the new covenant:

All your sons will be taught by the LORD (Isa. 54:13).
'The time is coming', declares the LORD, 'when I will make a new covenant with the house of Israel and with the house of Judah. It will not be like the covenant I made with their forefathers when I took them by the hand to lead them out of Egypt, because they broke my covenant, though I was a husband to them', declares the LORD... 'I will put my law in their minds and write it on their hearts. I will be their God, and they will be my people. No longer will a man teach his neighbour, or a man his brother, saying: "Know the LORD", because they will all know me, from the least of them to the greatest', declares the LORD. 'For I will forgive their wickedness and will remember their sins no more' (Jer. 31:31-34).
I will sprinkle clean water on you, and you will be clean; I will cleanse you from all your impurities and from all your idols. I will give you a new heart and put a new spirit in you; I will remove from you your heart of stone and give you a heart of flesh. And I will put my Spirit in you and move you to follow my decrees and be careful to keep my laws. You will live in the land I gave your forefathers; you will be my people, and I will be your God. I will save you from all your uncleanness (Ezek. 36:25-29; see also Ezek. 37:1-28; 39:21-29).

As Christ explained:

All that the Father gives me will come to me, and whoever comes to me I will never drive away. For I have come down from heaven not to do my will but to do the will of him who sent me. And this is the will of him who sent me, that I shall lose none of all that he has given me, but raise them up at the last day. For my Father's will is that everyone who looks to the Son and believes in him shall have eternal life, and I will raise him up at the last day... No one can come to me unless the Father who sent me draws him, and I will raise him up at the last day. It is written in the prophets: 'They will all be taught by God'. Everyone who listens to the Father and learns from him comes to me (John 6:37-45).

As the writer to the Hebrews told us:

The ministry Jesus has received is as superior to [that of the priests of the old covenant] as the covenant of which he is Mediator is superior to the old one, and it is founded on better promises. For if there had been nothing wrong with that first covenant, no place would have been sought for another. But God found fault with the people and said: 'The

time is coming', declares the Lord, 'when I will make a new covenant with the house of Israel and with the house of Judah. It will not be like the covenant I made with their forefathers when I took them by the hand to lead them out of Egypt, because they did not remain faithful to my covenant, and I turned away from them, declares the Lord. This is the covenant I will make with the house of Israel after that time, declares the Lord. I will put my laws in their minds and write them on their hearts. I will be their God, and they will be my people. No longer will a man teach his neighbour, or a man his brother, saying: "Know the Lord", because they will all know me, from the least of them to the greatest. For I will forgive their wickedness and will remember their sins no more'. By calling this covenant 'new', he has made the first one obsolete; and what is obsolete and ageing will soon disappear...
When this priest [Jesus] had offered for all time one sacrifice for sins, he sat down at the right hand of God. Since that time he waits for his enemies to be made his footstool, because by one sacrifice he has made perfect forever those who are being made holy. The Holy Spirit also testifies to us about this. First he says: 'This is the covenant I will make with them after that time', says the Lord. 'I will put my laws in their hearts, and I will write them on their minds'. Then he adds: 'Their sins and lawless acts I will remember no more'. And where these have been forgiven, there is no longer any sacrifice for sin (Heb. 8:6-13; 10:12-18).

And this work and witness of the Spirit in the believer can only lead to joy for the child of God. After all, we know that Christ had the Spirit, and joy through the Spirit. Luke recorded that 'Jesus [was] full of joy through the Holy Spirit' (Luke 10:21), that he 'rejoiced greatly in the Holy Spirit' (NASB). And this, surely, is the experience granted to believers: 'God has poured out his love into our hearts by the Holy Spirit, whom he has given us' (Rom. 5:5). This is how 'the disciples were filled with joy and with the Holy Spirit' (Acts 13:52). Can the believer not join with Mary: 'My spirit rejoices in God my Saviour' (Luke 1:47)? Paul, reminding the Thessalonians of their conversion, could say that they had 'welcomed the message with the joy given by the Holy Spirit' (1 Thess. 1:6).

And while I do not endorse everything about the way Spurgeon put it, nevertheless he made a valid point:

Brothers and sisters, let us learn our need of a personal revelation! Let us seek it if we have not yet received it! With a childlike spirit let us seek it in Christ, for only he can reveal the Father to us! And when we have it, let it be our joy that we see him revealing it to others and let this be our prayer, that the God of Jacob would yet bring others unto Christ who shall rejoice in the light of God that has made glad our eyes! The Lord be with you. Amen.[19]

Naturally, this witness of the Spirit, this sealing of the Spirit, this anointing of the Spirit, must exceed our comprehension, but we are told enough for us to come to an understanding of what we are talking about. It must be so! Believers have it! So let us look into it a little more.

Let me start by making a very important point, a negative point, but one which we must keep hold of when thinking about the witness of the Spirit.

The Spirit's witness is a continual experience
As I have already noted, the witness of the Spirit is not a one-off experience, something done and dusted. Right from the moment of our conversion, the Spirit witnesses with our spirit. Not only that. The Spirit goes on maintaining this witness throughout our entire earthly pilgrimage. How do we know this? By Paul's use of verbs: 'You did not receive a spirit that makes you a slave again to fear, but you received the Spirit of sonship. And by him we cry: "Abba, Father". The Spirit himself testifies with our spirit that we are God's children' (Rom. 8:15-16). We *received* (aorist tense) the Spirit at conversion (Rom. 8:15); that is, we received the Spirit as a one-off experience, with abiding effect. And it is as we *cry* (present tense, we go on crying), that the Spirit *bears witness* or *testifies* (present tense, the Spirit goes on witnessing), with us. In other words, the reception of the Spirit is an initial experience with abiding results. The Spirit resides in us, constantly carrying out his ministry within us: at conversion the Spirit removes our fear, confirms us as sons, enables us to call God our Father, and witnesses to us that we are Christ's, *and he continually goes on doing the same throughout the rest of our days*. In short, we are talking about a moment-by-moment authentication to our spirits, the Spirit assuring us, leading us to God through Christ and

---

[19] Sermon number 1571.

confirming our standing in Christ. Likewise, the Spirit seals us and anoints us, both the seal and the anointing being permanently ours.

And it is not only a question of the apostle's use of verbs. As I have explained, there is no break anywhere in Paul's statement in Romans 8:15-16, no suggestion of one. There is no break in the text, and there is no interlude between the believer's experience of the removal of his fear, his realisation that he is free to address God as his Father, his sense of sonship, and the witness of the Spirit. It is all one instantaneous and yet continuous episode, one encounter with God through Christ by the Spirit. It starts at conversion, and it abides. The Spirit deals with us in this way at the beginning, and he never stops dealing with us in this way. It is a present, not merely historical, experience for us.

Let me illustrate. While crossing the Atlantic, John Wesley, in contrast to his own sense of fear, had been deeply challenged by the courage and confidence displayed by the Moravians in the violent storm though which they had passed. On reaching Savannah, Georgia, he opened his heart to August Spangenberg, seeking his help. The Moravian responded: 'I must first ask you one or two questions'. Spangenberg wanted to know if Wesley was truly converted: 'Have you the witness within yourself? Does the Spirit of God bear witness with your spirit, that you are a child of God?' Wesley was stumped. 'Do you know Jesus Christ?' Spangenberg asked. Wesley replied: 'I know he is the Saviour of the world'. 'True', came the reply, 'but do you know he has saved you?' The best Wesley could say was: 'I hope he has died to save me'. Spangenberg: 'Do you know yourself?' Wesley: 'I do'. But, as Wesley later recorded in his Journal: 'I fear they were vain words'.

Spangenberg had shown Wesley that the Spirit's witness in bringing assurance was a mark of true faith. But now for the vital nuance. Pay careful attention to Spangenberg's questions (I am not playing with words): '*Have* you the witness within yourself? *Does* the Spirit of God bear witness with your spirit, that you *are* a child of God?' He did not ask: '*Did* you *have* an explosive one-off experience of the witness within yourself? *Did* the Spirit of God, in some sort of dramatic experience, bear witness with your spirit, that you *were* a child of God?'[20]

This is of such importance, I must stress it. Some look upon assurance, the witness of the Spirit, as a striking, one-off vision, sensation, mystical experience or whatever.[21] Lloyd-Jones, for one, certainly gave that impression, advocating the kind of experience he and various others – whom he citied, on more than once occasion and at length[22] – had enjoyed. *But this is not what the apostles were speaking of.* According to Scripture, the witness of the Spirit is a continual experience, an ever-present witness with our spirits, the Spirit continually taking away our fears, continually enabling us to call God our Father.

This witness of the Spirit is not to be likened to having one's appendix removed. A better comparison is with the way our

---

[20] George Whitefield reinforced this point when, in his letter which he wrote to John Wesley after the latter had published his sermon on predestination, he stated: 'For these five or six years, I have received [not 'I *did* receive'] the witness of the Spirit [I have made it upper case – DG]. Since then, blessed be God, I have not doubted a quarter of an hour of having a saving interest in Jesus Christ. But with grief and humble shame I do acknowledge I have fallen into sin often since that' (Gillies). For more from Whitefield, see below and Appendix 2.

[21] Gospel Standard Strict Baptists are mistakenly waiting for a manifestation of their eternal justification (actual justification in eternity past) as one of the elect, this being their 'conversion' and assurance rolled in one (see my *Eternal*; *No Safety*). As can be seen from the Gospel Standard Articles, the witness of the Spirit is the very acme of Christian experience: 'We believe that there are various degrees of faith, as little faith and great faith ; that when a man is quickened by the blessed Spirit, he has faith given him to know and feel that he is a sinner against God, and that without a Saviour he must sink in black despair. And we further believe that such a man will be made to cry for mercy, to mourn over and on account of his sins, and, being made to feel that he has no righteousness of his own, to hunger and thirst after Christ's righteousness; being led on by the Spirit until, in the full assurance of faith, he has the Spirit's witness in his heart that his sins are for ever put away'. Unfortunately, J.H.Gosden in his definitive commentary on the articles, when commenting on the article in question (number 35), said nothing about the witness of the Spirit.

[22] See, for instance, Lloyd-Jones: *Preaching* pp315-324; *Joy* pp105-107,112-113,125; *Sons* pp315-360.

ductless glands work, with the way we breathe, or with the beating of our pulse, something which is going on all the time, and – when all is well – free of dramatic sensation. The illustration, I confess, is poor, but we must get away from the notion of assurance as some sort of vivid one-off explosion, a crisis, or the switching on of a light, and hold to the idea of a continual basking in the enjoyment of the warming rays of the sun.

If we do look upon the witness of the Spirit as some sort of mystical occurrence or dramatic encounter, we run the risk of relying on that experience. If so, we will be placing our confidence entirely in the wrong place, and on the wrong object; namely, on experience, rather than on Christ. This is a mistake of immense proportions. The Spirit bears witness to Christ – to Christ – not to himself, not to his gifts, nor to some phenomenon or incident which we look back on.

The same may be said of conversion. We must not draw our assurance from the circumstances of our conversion. As I said, assurance does not arise from the historical; it arises in the 'today', the present, the here and now. It's not what happened to me on a certain date (which I may know – or think I know!). What really matters is the preciousness of Christ to me at this very moment, and the reality of my walk with him today. Peter tells us: 'To you who believe, [the Lord Jesus Christ] is precious' (1 Pet. 2:7). He does not say that Christ *was* precious to you on a certain date – maybe long in the past – as an experience you look back upon with fond and somewhat faded memory, *and that is all*. Christ became precious to you then, yes, but he *is* precious to you *now*. This is assurance.

There is a parallel with Christ's ordinances: baptism and the Lord's supper. Both are symbolic. Both speak of Christ and the believer's relationship to him. Baptism represents and speaks of the sinner's conversion, his union with Christ as he comes to faith.[23] And baptism is undergone once by the believer, and once only: he is dipped, immersed, as a representation and declaration of his union with Christ and of his being washed in the blood of Christ.

---

[23] Rom. 6:3-4 speaks of the believer's actual union with Christ by spiritual baptism. Although Paul is not speaking about water baptism in that passage (see my *Hinge*), water baptism certainly represents it.

But the believer observes the Lord's supper repeatedly – 'as often as you eat this bread and drink this cup' (1 Cor. 11:26, NKJV) – and this speaks of his constant feeding upon Christ, his unending rest in Christ, his continual cleansing in the blood of Christ (1 John 1:9).[24] Thus the believer is saved at his conversion, and is being saved continually.[25] It takes the two ordinances to fully speak of this once-for-all and yet conscious moment-by-moment experience of salvation in, through and by Christ. That, of course, is why Christ gave both of them to us. So it is with the witness of the Spirit. The Spirit is not only given to the sinner in his conversion, and witnesses to him at that time, but, residing with the believer throughout his pilgrimage, he is always actively bearing witness with the believer, always confirming him as a child of God.

To sum up: the believer does not rest on any event – conversion or some supposed mystical experience which he may call 'the witness of the Spirit'. No! He rests on Christ. He rests entirely and only on Christ for his justification, he rests on Christ for his assurance, he rests on Christ for his sanctification, he rests on Christ for his liberty, he rests on Christ for his glory, he rests on Christ only and entirely for his all: 'Christ is all' (Col. 3:11). 'Christ is all' is not a slogan. For the believer, it is a reality: 'Christ is all'.

And this is the very area in which the Spirit works. Day by day, he takes of the things of Christ, takes of the person of Christ himself, and makes Christ, and all that belongs to Christ, to be known and felt by the believer. In this way, the Spirit unceasingly enables the child of God to sense the glory of his Redeemer (John 14:16-17,26; 15:26; 16:7,13-15), and to enjoy the thought that Christ is his (John 5:11; Rom. 5:2,11; 14:17; Phil. 3:3; 1 Pet. 1:6,8, for instance). This is the witness of the Spirit. And one of the fruits of the Spirit is joy (Gal. 5:22).

But is there no danger in all this talk of the Spirit? As with every aspect of the new covenant, the answer must be: Yes, of course. Even so, unless we expose ourselves to this danger, to this

---

[24] This verse is written to believers, don't forget.
[25] He is also saved in eternity past in God's decree, and will be finally and utterly saved in eternity to come (see my *Eternal*).

accusation, we are not thinking and speaking biblically.[26] Some believers, however, dwelling on this danger, might raise two objections.

Two objections answered

Is there not a danger in this emphasis on the Spirit? Moreover, what will prevent a believer deluding himself that his own feelings are indeed the witness of the Spirit?

These are serious objections. In reply, we need to remember that I have drawn my doctrine that assurance comes primarily by the witness of the Spirit and not by sanctification – which, I admit will seem to be excessive and strange to many today – directly from the New Testament. I have been quoting Christ and his apostles. And the New Testament always speaks of the work of the Spirit in the highest terms, and speaks unequivocally, even to the extent that no member of the new covenant needs a human teacher. Take, for example, these statements – which are true of every believer:

No longer will a man teach his neighbour, or a man his brother, saying: 'Know the Lord', because they will all know me, from the least of them to the greatest (Heb. 8:11).
You have an anointing from the Holy One, and all of you know the truth. I do not write to you because you do not know the truth, but because you do know it and because no lie comes from the truth... As for you, the anointing you received from him remains in you, and you do not need anyone to teach you. But as his anointing teaches you about all things and as that anointing is real, not counterfeit – just as it has taught you, remain in him (1 John 2:20-21,27).

Clearly, these verses cannot possibly mean what they appear to be saying at first glance. After all, both John and the writer to the Hebrews were teaching as they were saying it; in fact, they were writing Scripture. But, even so, the promise still stands.

---

[26] Let me explain: preaching free grace always leads to accusation of antinomianism (Rom. 6:1-2). Unless men can accuse us of it, therefore, we are not preaching the gospel properly. Likewise with assurance. Unless men can accuse us of over-emphasising the Spirit, we are not preaching biblically on the matter. We must leave ourselves open to the accusation of antinomianism. See below for the 17th century New England crisis.

And herein lies the key to the answer to the question as to how we are to avoid the pitfall of relying on mere feeling. Do not miss my use of 'mere'. Feeling is essential! There's far too much sterility and dryness about these days! The key to all this, however, is the balance we must maintain between the Spirit and the word. It is not a question of the Spirit or the Scriptures; it is not the Spirit above the Scriptures; it is the Spirit and the Scriptures! Indeed, as we have seen repeatedly, in the new covenant God gives all his people the Spirit, he writes his law – the gospel, Christ – on their hearts, and he, at the same time, gives them the Scriptures.[27] The believer, therefore, is under all three: the Spirit, the law written in his heart and the Scriptures, all three of them mutually calibrating each other, and all three stirring the believer to assurance and sanctification.

So, how do we know that believers have the witness of the Spirit? Because the Bible tells us so! How are believers able to understand, enjoy and obey the Scriptures, and, above all, find Christ in them? Because they have the gospel, Christ, written on their hearts. How do they weigh their feelings? By the law of Christ in their heart and by the written word. It is the word and the Spirit – not the Spirit above the word. But neither is it the word above the Spirit![28] It is word and Spirit, the word written on the heart by the Spirit. So, while there is always a danger of coming down on one side or the other – the word or the Spirit – it has to be both.

So much for the objections.

But that digression leads me to the ultimate point. I have hinted at it in passing, but it is time for me to set it out more fully.

And what, especially, does the Spirit witness to us about?

It's not a 'what'! It's a 'whom!' Christ! As he himself told us, the supreme work of the Spirit is to take of the things of the Lord Jesus and make them known to believers, and so to glorify the Saviour. In other words, by making Christ known to believers, and doing so more and more, the Spirit confirms and assures them of their

---

[27] As just *one* example, link Rom. 8:1-4,9 with Gal. 6:2 and 2 Tim. 3:15-16. See my *Christ* for my argument.

[28] I will return to this when speaking of 'legal assurance'.

standing in Christ. He does this by witnessing to them about the person and the name of Christ, his love for sinners, his work for sinners, his blood shed for sinners. But not only that! It gets far more personal, praise God! The Spirit speaks to *us* about the person and the name of Christ, his love for *us*, his work for *us*, his blood shed for *us*. Above all, every believer can say the Spirit witnesses to *me*, and tells *me* of the person and the name of Christ, his love for *me*, his work for *me*, his blood shed for *me*.

By way of example, I have already quoted Galatians 2:20, in which Paul shows how he appropriated Christ by the Spirit: 'The Son of God... loved me and gave himself for me' (Gal. 2:20). Now for some further testimonies. Consider the following scriptures:

Jesus our Lord... was delivered over to death for our sins and was raised to life for our justification (Rom. 4:24-25).

Therefore, since we have been justified through faith, we have peace with God through our Lord Jesus Christ, through whom we have gained access by faith into this grace in which we now stand. And we rejoice in the hope of the glory of God... And hope does not disappoint us, because God has poured out his love into our hearts by the Holy Spirit, whom he has given us... God demonstrates his own love for us in this: While we were still sinners, Christ died for us. Since we have now been justified by his blood, how much more shall we be saved from God's wrath through him! For if, when we were God's enemies, we were reconciled to him through the death of his Son, how much more, having been reconciled, shall we be saved through his life! Not only is this so, but we also rejoice in God through our Lord Jesus Christ, through whom we have now received reconciliation (Rom. 5:1-5,8-11).

God, who said: 'Let light shine out of darkness', made his light shine in our hearts to give us the light of the knowledge of the glory of God in the face of Christ (2 Cor. 4:6).

You know the grace of our Lord Jesus Christ, that though he was rich, yet for your sakes he became poor, so that you through his poverty might become rich (2 Cor. 8:9).

The Spirit takes those scriptures – and all like them – and underscores the personal – to *me*:

Jesus *my* Lord... was delivered over to death for *my* sins and was raised to life for *my* justification (Rom. 4:24-25).

Therefore, since *I* have been justified through faith, *I* have peace with God through our Lord Jesus Christ, through whom *I* have gained

access by faith into this grace in which *I* now stand. And *I* rejoice in
the hope of the glory of God... And hope does not disappoint *me*,
because God has poured out his love into *my* heart by the Holy Spirit,
whom he has given *me*... God demonstrates his own love for *me* in this:
While *I* was still a sinner, Christ died for *me*. Since *I* have now been
justified by his blood, how much more shall *I* be saved from God's
wrath through him! For if, when *I* was one of God's enemies, *I* was
reconciled to him through the death of his Son, how much more,
having been reconciled, shall *I* be saved through his life! Not only is
this so, but *I* also rejoice in God through our Lord Jesus Christ, through
whom *I* have now received reconciliation (Rom. 5:1-5,8-11).
God, who said: 'Let light shine out of darkness', made his light shine
in *my* heart to give *me* the light of the knowledge of the glory of God in
the face of Christ (2 Cor. 4:6).
You know the grace of our Lord Jesus Christ, that though he was rich,
yet for *my* sake he became poor, so that *I* through his poverty might
become rich (2 Cor. 8:9).

And so on. And it is this witness of the Spirit, enabling us to speak
in such personal terms, that gives us assurance.

The glory of Christ, the uniqueness of Christ, the fact that Christ
is all – is the constant refrain of the New Testament (John 13:31-
32; 17:1-5,24; 2 Cor. 4:1-6; Col. 1:27; 3:11; 2 Thess. 2:14; Heb.
13:21; 2 Pet. 3:18, and so on). Right at the start of his public
ministry, as Jesus was baptised, God announced: 'This is my Son,
whom I love; with him I am well pleased' (Matt. 3:17). The Greeks
demanded to see Jesus (John 12:21) – and the Spirit makes sure
believers do see him! By the Spirit (John 15:26; 16:13-15), Peter,
James and John never forgot the lesson they learned at Jesus'
transfiguration. Peter might think of equating Christ with Moses
(the law) and Elijah (the prophets), but the Father let him know
how mistaken he was, and in no uncertain terms: the cloud
immediately descended, blotting everything out. When they could
see again, Moses and Elijah had been removed, leaving Christ to
stand alone. And then God spoke: 'This is my Son, whom I love;
with him I am well pleased. Listen to him!' So: 'When they looked
up, they saw no one except Jesus' (Matt. 17:5-8). As I say, Peter
never forgot it:

We did not follow cleverly invented stories when we told you about
the power and coming of our Lord Jesus Christ, but we were
eyewitnesses of his majesty. For he received honour and glory from

God the Father when the voice came to him from the majestic glory, saying: 'This is my Son, whom I love; with him I am well pleased'. We ourselves heard this voice that came from heaven when we were with him on the sacred mountain. And we have the word of the prophets made more certain, and you will do well to pay attention to it, as to a light shining in a dark place, until the day dawns and the morning star rises in your hearts (2 Pet. 1:16-19).[29]

All this speaks volumes. The Spirit's work is to magnify Christ; to magnify Christ, I stress. There's no cult of the Spirit here. We are talking about 'the Spirit of Christ' (Rom. 8:9). There are only two places in all Scripture where the Holy Spirit is called 'the Spirit of Christ': here and 1 Peter 1:11.[30] Is it not significant that Paul used the phrase – uniquely for him – when leading up to the witness of the Spirit to the child of God? Notice also the parallel expression in the corresponding passage in Galatians: 'Because you are sons, God sent *the Spirit of his Son into our [your] hearts*, the Spirit who calls out: "Abba, Father"' (Gal. 4:6). Nothing could be clearer. The Spirit of Christ bears witness to the believer, and bears witness by pointing him to Christ, and glorifying Christ to him. And this is the believer's assurance, just as the Spirit himself is the believer's seal (2 Cor. 1:21-22; Eph. 1:13-14). 'To [those] who believe, [the Lord Jesus Christ] is precious' (1 Pet. 2:7).[31]

James Dunn:

---

[29] In his second letter, how many times did Peter mention the Spirit? How many times did he refer to the written word of God (not forgetting allusions)? How many times did he refer to Christ? The answer to the first is once; the second and third, I gave up counting! Notice how Peter brought his letter to a close: 'Bear in mind that our Lord's patience means salvation, just as our dear brother Paul also *wrote* you with the wisdom that God gave him. He *writes* the same way in all his *letters*, speaking in them of these matters. His *letters* contain some things that are hard to understand, which ignorant and unstable people distort, as they do the other *scriptures*, to their own destruction. Therefore, dear friends, since you already know this, be on your guard so that you may not be carried away by the error of lawless men and fall from your secure position. But grow in the grace and knowledge of *our Lord and Saviour Jesus Christ*. To him be glory both now and forever! Amen' (2 Pet. 3:15-18). No emphasis on the Spirit, please note.

[30] But see also 1 Cor. 12:3; 15:45; 2 Cor. 3:18; Gal. 4:6; Phil. 1:19.

[31] I will return to this scripture.

It is fundamental to this role of the Spirit as the Spirit of sonship that the Spirit is also the Spirit of the Son. Indeed, the Spirit is the Spirit of sonship precisely because [he] is the Spirit of the Son. That is to say, the Spirit for Paul links the believer directly to Jesus; the Spirit defines the person as [a] Christian precisely by establishing this link. And [he] makes this plain by reproducing the prayer relation of Jesus himself with God in believers: like Jesus, believers cry 'Abba, Father'. and thus attest that they are children of God and joint heirs with Christ (Rom. 8:16-17)... Notable is the interaction of divine Spirit and human spirit. Divine voice and human voice: the Spirit 'by whom we cry "Abba, Father" [and thereby][32] the same Spirit bears witness with our spirit that we are God's children' (Rom. 8:15-16); 'having the firstfruits of the Spirit we ourselves groan within ourselves (Rom. 8:23); 'the Spirit [himself] intercedes on our behalf with inarticulate groans, and he who searches the hearts knows that is the Spirit's way of thinking' (Rom. 8:26-27). In the intensity of prayer and abandonment to God in what would otherwise be total human despair, Spirit speech and heart language become as one.[33]

And 1 Peter 1:10-11 has something to say in this regard:

Concerning this salvation, the prophets, who spoke of the grace that was to come to you, searched intently and with the greatest care, trying to find out the time and circumstances to which the Spirit of Christ in them was pointing when he predicted the sufferings of Christ and the glories that would follow.

Peter uses the phrase 'the Spirit of Christ' when he wants to speak of the Spirit's work in directing the prophets to... to what? To Christ and his work of salvation. The parallel is unmistakable.

In short: Christ, not the Spirit, is the focus of attention. And this is at the heart of the new covenant. In what follows, do not miss the link between the Spirit and Christ, but, equally, do not miss where the emphasis lies; namely, Christ:

Therefore, there is now no condemnation for those who are in Christ Jesus, because through Christ Jesus the law of the Spirit of life set me free from the law of sin and death. For what the law was powerless to do in that it was weakened by the flesh, God did by sending his own Son in the likeness of sinful man to be a sin offering. And so he condemned sin in sinful man, in order that the righteous requirements

---

[32] Brackets original.
[33] Dunn: 'Spirit' pp84,91.

of the law might be fully met in us, who do not live according to the flesh but according to the Spirit. Those who live according to the flesh have their minds set on what that nature desires; but those who live in accordance with the Spirit have their minds set on what the Spirit desires. The mind of sinful man is death, but the mind controlled by the Spirit is life and peace; the sinful mind is hostile to God. It does not submit to God's law, nor can it do so. Those controlled by the flesh cannot please God. You, however, are controlled not by the flesh but by the Spirit, if the Spirit of God lives in you. And if anyone does not have the Spirit of Christ, he does not belong to Christ. But if Christ is in you, your body is dead because of sin, yet your spirit is alive because of righteousness. And if the Spirit of him who raised Jesus from the dead is living in you, he who raised Christ from the dead will also give life to your mortal bodies through his Spirit, who lives in you. Therefore, brothers, we have an obligation – but it is not to the flesh, to live according to it. For if you live according to the flesh, you will die; but if by the Spirit you put to death the misdeeds of the body, you will live, because those who are led by the Spirit of God are sons of God. For you did not receive a spirit that makes you a slave again to fear, but you received the Spirit of sonship. And by him we cry: 'Abba, Father'. The Spirit himself testifies with our spirit that we are God's children. Now if we are children, then we are heirs – heirs of God and co-heirs with Christ, if indeed we share in his sufferings in order that we may also share in his glory (Rom. 8:1-17).[34]

Again, consider the exchange between Jesus and his disciples as he approached the cross. He told them: 'I am with you for only a short time, and then I go to the one who sent me. You will look for me, but you will not find me; and where I am, you cannot come' (John 7:33-34). As his sufferings drew ever nearer, Christ told the crowds: 'You are going to have the light just a little while longer. Walk while you have the light, before darkness overtakes you. The man who walks in the dark does not know where he is going. Put your trust in the light while you have it, so that you may become sons of light' (John 12:35-36). He reminded his disciples of the sad news that he was leaving them: 'My children, I will be with you only a little longer. You will look for me, and just as I told the Jews, so I tell you now: Where I am going, you cannot come' (John

---

[34] It's not just here. We see the same throughout Romans. Nothing must get in the way of Christ. Not even talk of the Spirit. See Rom. 6:1-12; 12:1 – 15:13. And it's not just Romans!

13:31). On learning of this, the disciples were afraid and sorrowful (John 14:1,27; 16:6,22). But Jesus reassured them. To their amazement (I am sure), his departure would make things even better for them: 'I will not leave you as orphans; I will come to you' (John 13:31; 14:18). 'It is for your good [advantage, NASB] that I am going away. Unless I go away, the Counsellor will not come to you; but if I go, I will send him to you' (John 16:7). And the Spirit, once he had come, would never leave them: 'I will ask the Father, and he will give you another Counsellor to be with you for ever – the Spirit of truth' (John 14:16-17).

There's a depth of meaning in all this. The disciples knew that Christ was the Son of God and spoke the words of eternal life, Peter's confession being poignant in the extreme: 'Lord, to whom shall we go? You have the words of eternal life' (John 6:68-69). What would they do, how would they manage, without Jesus with them to counsel and teach them? And yet the Lord said it would be better for them after he had gone! The Spirit would come! Whatever could he mean?

Now, whatever a counsellor and companion does, he talks, doesn't he? Have you ever been in a room with somebody who will not speak? I stress the 'will not'. The gentle silence of companionship is precious; the wilful silence of barely disguised enmity or separation is grim. Such silence is not reassuring. It is oppressive, sullen, hurtful. The Spirit does not reside with his people to be silent! And he's more than *with* his people! He is *in* them! As Jesus said: 'He lives with you and will be in you' (John 14:17). And a vital part of his ministry is to bear witness to the believer, to talk to him and with him, giving him the words of eternal life. When Christ said: 'The Spirit gives life; the flesh counts for nothing. The words I have spoken to you are spirit and they are life' (John 6:63), coupled with: 'The Spirit of truth... he will testify about me... He will guide you into all truth... He will bring glory to me by taking from what is mine and making it known to you' (John 15:26; 16:13-14), he surely meant that the Spirit would continue Jesus' ministry within believers, even when the Lord was no longer with them in person.

When the two disciples on the Emmaus road were depressed, Jesus joined them and took away their sadness. How? By speaking to them, speaking to them about himself, about his sufferings and his glory, and doing so out of the Scriptures (Luke 24:13-35). This is precisely the way in which the Spirit witnesses to us and with us as believers, and gives us assurance: he shows us Christ, Christ in his sufferings, and present and future glory – and the Spirit makes us know that it is all for us.

Thus the Spirit goes on assuring us, leading us to Christ. It is as we *continue* to see more of Christ, the more the Spirit *makes* us continue to feel and enjoy our interest in the Redeemer, even increasing our joy and sense of glory and enabling us to live more Christ-like in this fallen world: 'Where the Spirit of the Lord is, there is freedom. And we, who with unveiled faces all reflect the Lord's glory, are being transformed into his likeness with ever-increasing glory, which comes from the Lord, who is the Spirit' (2 Cor. 3:17-18). Thus we fulfil Peter's command: 'Grow in the grace and knowledge of our Lord and Saviour Jesus Christ. To him be glory both now and forever! Amen' (2 Pet. 3:18). This is the Spirit's great work in the believer, day by day.

Anticipating what is to come, relying on evidences, works, sanctification for assurance is to rely on shifting sand. Christ is the believer's assurance! 'Jesus Christ is the same yesterday and today and for ever' (Heb. 13:8). 'All may change, but Jesus never'. The Spirit bears witness to Christ, and he bears witness to us about Christ. The weight of the Spirit's witness falls not on the gift – the Spirit – but on the giver – Christ. And herein lies the root of our assurance: Christ! He is the very substance and centre of it all. Of it all, I say.[35] Christ is all![36]

---

[35] Take sanctification. Take the last three chapters of Ephesians, and see how often the apostle links his commands for godliness to the person and work of Christ. See my series: 'Thoughts On Ephesians' (David H J Gay Ministry sermonaudio.com).

[36] 'Oh, that's verging on antinomianism!' That's how some dismiss what I have set before you, reader: 'Antinomianism!' Let them! Believer, in Christ you *are* sinless in Christ – not in yourself, but in Christ. You *are* marked in Christ. It is because of Christ, and through Christ, and with Christ, that you are marked with a seal. God stamps you with his mark: 'This is mine! This man, this woman, is mine. This believer is my son, my daughter, my child, my adopted child. He has my Son's righteousness clothing him. I see him as righteous as Jesus. I love him immeasurably – as

As we listen to Paul's prayers for believers, we can surely see the part played by the Spirit in his witness to the children of God:

I keep asking that the God of our Lord Jesus Christ, the glorious Father, may give you the Spirit of wisdom and revelation, so that you may know him better. I pray also that the eyes of your heart may be enlightened in order that you may know the hope to which he has called you, the riches of his glorious inheritance in the saints, and his incomparably great power for us who believe... I pray that out of his glorious riches he may strengthen you with power through his Spirit in your inner being, so that Christ may dwell in your hearts through faith. And I pray that you, being rooted and established in love, may have power, together with all the saints, to grasp how wide and long and high and deep is the love of Christ, and to know this love that surpasses knowledge – that you may be filled to the measure of all the fullness of God. Now to him who is able to do immeasurably more than all we ask or imagine, according to his power that is at work within us, to him be glory in the church and in Christ Jesus throughout all generations, for ever and ever! Amen (Eph. 1:17-19; 3:16-21).

This is New Testament assurance.

Stibbs and Packer will bring this chapter to a close:

Throughout the New Testament it is taken for granted that Christians are joyfully certain of their standing in God's grace, their sonship in his family, and their hope of his glory – all the good things, in fact, which are spelled out in sequence as belonging to 'us' – Paul and all his Christian readers – in chapter 8 of the letter to the Romans. Whence came this certainty? From the ministry – that is, from the attitudes, convictions and habits which he implanted. It was the Spirit who gave those first Christians confidence and liberty, and made it their deepest instinct to call on God as 'Father'; and, writes Paul: 'When we cry: "Abba, Father"... it is the Spirit himself bearing witness with our spirit that we are children of God' (Rom. 8:15f; see also Gal. 4:6).. Earlier in Romans he had written that the love of God, as shown forth at the cross, 'has been poured into our hearts through the Holy Spirit who has been given to us' (Rom. 5:5)... 'By this we know that he

---

I love my Son. I love him without end. And this child of mine, this sealed and adopted child of mine, shall be brought to everlasting glory'. And it's the work of the Spirit to bear witness of all this to you, believer, and to confirm and assure you of all that you have in the Lord Jesus. He does this by making Jesus more and more precious to you (1 Pet. 2:7).

abides in us, by the Spirit he gave us'... 'By this we know that we abide in him and he in us, because he has given us of his own Spirit' (1 John 3:24; 4:13)...

Moreover, the gift of the indwelling Spirit, of which Christians become aware in the manner described by discovering the change that the Spirit has wrought in them, is intended to assure Christians of their future resurrection and glory with Christ, no less than their present standing in grace through Christ... (2 Cor. 5:1-5)... (Eph. 1:13f).

Finally, a most important observation made by Stibbs and Packer, one which will take us into the next chapter:

It appears that so far from the present enjoyment of assurance indicating that one is presumptuous, conceited, and self-deceived, the non-enjoyment of it proclaims an unhealthy and sub-normal spiritual condition. It appears, too, that those who oppose the teaching and decry the experience of assurance are themselves guilty of presumption and conceit, in their audacious preference for anti-scriptural doctrine.[37]

And that leads us to think a little more about why so many of today's believers are prone to doubt.

But just before I leave this chapter, let me return to the way I opened it, drawing attention to the simplicity and brevity of the New Testament on assurance. Since I have so clearly broken my own rubric, let me restate the apostolic teaching on this vital matter. If we want to know the way of assurance, all we have to do is read and appropriate Romans 8:9,14-17,23; 2 Corinthians 1:21-22; 5:5; Galatians 4:6-7; Ephesians 1:13-14; 4:30; 1 John 2:20-27; 3:24; 4:13; 5:6,9-11. It's all there. And in a nutshell, at that.

---

[37] Stibbs and Packer pp87-89. For comments from other writers in support of what I have set out, see Appendix 2.

Why Do Believers Doubt?

Note the title! Yes, true believers can doubt. Sadly, it is so. It ought not to be, but it's one of those stubborn facts of life – one which will not go away simply by wishing it so. Accommodating the words of Christ (Matt. 26:11; Mark 14:7; John 12:8), it seems we have to accept that 'we will always have the unassured among us'. Why is this? Why do *believers* doubt? As I have explained, one reason is that many are on the wrong spiritual diet. Just as a lack of vitamin D and calcium can produce rickets in children, so misdirected or bad teaching can lead to all sorts of spiritual maladies for believers, including doubt and excessive introspection. Some of it stems from the misinformed preaching they heard before they were converted, and then go on hearing after their conversion. Downright error, of course, will be even more devastating! It happened in the New Testament. And that is why Paul and John (and others) wrote to certain believers – Paul confronting the Judaisers, and Paul and John the proto-Gnostics.[1] Take Paul, writing to the Colossians:

So then, just as you received Christ Jesus as Lord, continue to live in him, rooted and built up in him, strengthened in the faith as you were taught, and overflowing with thankfulness. See to it that no one takes you captive through hollow and deceptive philosophy, which depends on human tradition and the basic principles of this world rather than on Christ (Col. 2:6-8).

Here is Paul's argument: believers have a responsibility. As he tells us: 'See to it that no one takes you captive'. 'See to it'! Captive? Literally, 'makes a prey of you', from the verb *sulagōgeō*, 'to carry

---

[1] Gnosticism is very difficult to tie down. Although it flourished from about the 2nd century, the early church faced it in embryo. It involves denial of the true humanity of Christ, a special 'knowledge' available only to the elite, and a tendency to antinomianism. John wrote to deal with it in his day. But notice that John, in prosecuting his argument against Gnosticism and antinomianism did not once mention the law, let alone draw on what would become Calvin's third use of it. Just in case it needs saying, 1 John 2:3; 3:22-24; 5:3 do not refer to the law of Moses.

off as a captive or slave'; here, 'to make a slave of by false teaching'. 'See to it that no one takes you captive *through hollow and deceptive philosophy*, which depends on human tradition and the basic principles of this world rather than on Christ'. Here is the point: false teaching, if imbibed and followed, enslaves true believers. And what does slavery produce? Fear, loss of hope, grief, sorrow, and such like.

This passage is not unique. Consider the following:

I urge you, brothers, to watch out for those who cause divisions and *put obstacles in your way* that are contrary to the teaching you have learned. Keep away from them. For such people are not serving our Lord Christ, but their own appetites. By smooth talk and flattery they *deceive the minds* of naïve people (Rom. 16:17-18).
I am afraid that just as Eve was *deceived* by the serpent's cunning, *your minds* may somehow be *led astray* from your sincere and pure devotion to Christ (2 Cor. 11:3).
Some people are throwing you into *confusion* and are trying to pervert the gospel of Christ (Gal. 1:7).
There are many rebellious people, mere talkers and *deceivers*, especially those of the circumcision group. They must be silenced, because they are *ruining* whole households by teaching things they ought not to teach (Tit. 1:10-11).

I think the case is made. False teaching brings bondage, and bondage brings loss of assurance and joy.[2]

---

[2] Take 1 Cor. 8:9. This has nothing to do with assurance, but note how believers can be badly affected by what they see other believers doing. In light of this, think how bad *teaching* might cause true believers to stumble. Gill: The apostle tells believers who knew they had liberty that 'they ought to be cautious, lest they should be the means of offending, or causing to offend, such who were weak in the faith, and had not that knowledge of Christian liberty they had. Not [that] the use of their power and liberty is here denied, but the abuse of it is guarded against... being attended with very bad consequences'. Matthew Henry spoke of 'the mischief such freedom might do to weaker Christians, persons that had not the same measure of knowledge... Weak Christians may be ignorant, or have but a confused knowledge of the greatest and plainest truths... They were weak in their understanding... contracted... guilt... and so greatly polluted themselves... We should be careful to do nothing that may occasion weak Christians to defile their consciences'. See also Rom. 14 – 15. The principle applies to teaching.

Paul, we know, was deeply concerned about the Galatians and their loss of joy (Gal. 4:15), and, as John told us, one of the reasons behind his writing his first letter was to bring the believers back into the joy and assurance they had lost.[3] How had the Galatians lost their joy? By listening to the law preachers. How had John's readers lost their joy? By listening to the Gnostics. And so on. The first believers all had the witness of the Spirit at their conversion. But some of them lost their joy – and their assurance – through false teaching.

Now come to our time. We live in the culture of inclusivism induced by Christendom. In saying this, I am speaking about the churches, not merely society. What am I talking about? By 'inclusivism', I mean the way in which we treat unbelievers in our churches, assemblies or meetings, addressing them as believers.[4] It takes many and varied forms, but I am thinking, for instance, of the ambience of 'friendship-evangelism'. Where such an atmosphere of inclusivism prevails, preaching to sinners is severely muted, and the way sinners are dealt with is fundamentally changed. In all this, we radically depart from the New Testament. Unbelievers, under such a system, are badly damaged, deluded as to the way of salvation, and possibly deceived to their eternal ruin. Do we not see the evidence all around us, staring us in the face? This evidence – the production of many unconverted professors (Ishmaels not Isaacs as one old saint called them) – can only increase the longer it goes on. The harvest will be grim, not only for the individuals concerned, but for the churches. As for those who are genuinely converted under such a system, is it surprising that many of them, as it were, suffer birth damage as a result of mishandling at the point of conversion? We know of the consequences of such mistreatment in the physical realm. Does the same not apply in the spiritual realm?

Now think of those who are existing in an atmosphere of (overt or incipient) law teaching, including preparationism, where they are taught by men who never mention the witness of the Spirit, or, perhaps refer to it only to stress that the experience is beyond the reach of most believers. And say this has been going for decades, if not centuries? It is surely not surprising that such people, if they are

---

[3] In Appendix 3, I justify these claims with regard to 1 John.

[4] See my *Infant* pp271-274,292; *Baptist* pp327-332; *Glorious* pp186-195.

genuinely converted, nevertheless are totally confused about the witness of the Spirit – if they think about it at all. The effect that this must have on assurance is patent.

How can we help believers who are struggling with lack of assurance because of this kind of teaching? Unless we are prepared to say that those who do not have a clear experience and understanding of the witness of the Spirit are not converted,[5] that assurance is an essential mark of faith,[6] then we must have a way of helping *true believers* who are so damaged.

And many are damaged in this way. If we live on a diet of misguided (or worse) teaching, one in which we are constantly given the legal view of assurance,[7] and told how it is virtually impossible for us ever to get assurance, and it can hardly be wondered that loss of joy will be our inevitable lot!

This is such a vital matter, let me substantiate it by one or two more illustrations. Have you heard of Émile Coué de la Châtaigneraie? A French psychologist, living from 1857-1926, Coué gave the world 'the Coué method', in which a patient repeats the mantra: 'Every day, in every way, I am getting better and better'. The patient says this to himself daily, twenty times a day, including first thing in the morning and last thing at night. And to a certain extent it works. The idea, repeated and reinforced, becomes a reality. I suggest that if believers are reared on a diet of legal preaching, where they are told repeatedly that sanctification is the way to assurance, told repeatedly that introspection is the key, and told repeatedly that even so the struggle will probably be fruitless – a kind of dark Couéism, Couéism in reverse – it can hardly be surprising if believers end up lacking assurance.

Put it to the test on a related issue. We know that the believer, as he comes to faith, is united to Christ, dies to the law, and is delivered from the law. This, beyond question, is the plain teaching of the New Testament, especially Romans 6 – 8.[8] Very well. Imagine a teacher who insists – and keeps insisting – that in order

---

[5] Which some people do say.

[6] See Appendix 1.

[7] I will fully explain my terms, and justify my claims, in the following chapter.

[8] See my *Christ* for all my supporting evidence.

to die to the law, and be liberated from the law, believers must struggle for it, long for it, pray for it, seek it, agonise for it – over many years – but continually warns his hearers and readers that most of them will never get there. What do you think will be the effect on his hearers?

So it is with assurance. If believers are taught by one who never mentions assurance by the witness of the Spirit – let alone argues for it from Scripture – or tells them that it comes only to the favoured few, and then only after a protracted and tormenting struggle – is it likely that such unfortunate believers will become assured? This preacher, probably wrestling with his own lack of assurance, is hardly best placed to help others beset by the same difficulty.

And a ministry lacking a proper emphasis on the Spirit is not fanciful! It can happen. It has happened. Remember the men at Ephesus:

While Apollos was at Corinth, Paul took the road through the interior and arrived at Ephesus. There he found some disciples and asked them: 'Did you receive the Holy Spirit when you believed?' They answered: 'No, we have not even heard that there is a Holy Spirit' (Acts 19:1-2).

How did that manifest itself do you think?

Here's another illustration. Do you remember Hiroo Onoda – that Japanese soldier who was found in the jungle – the one who for almost thirty years did not know that the Second World War had finished in 1945, or at least refused to believe it? He had seen a leaflet telling him the war was over, but he wouldn't believe it – and he remained in bondage, fighting a lost cause.

What about us today? I am saying that many believers are taught into a lack of assurance. Instead of listening to the Spirit – maybe the 'still small voice' or 'gentle whisper' (1 Kings 19:12), or 'whisper divine'[9] – they listen to the strident warnings of those who tell them again and again that assurance is only really possible to

---

[9] J.Stocker: 'Great Father of mercies, thy goodness I own,/ And the covenant love of thy crucified Son;/ All praise to the Spirit, whose whisper divine/ Seals mercy, and pardon, and righteousness mine' (*Gospel Hymns* number 51).

the favoured few, and that after years of struggle. This *is* happening today.

Just a minute! Isn't the Spirit sovereign? He overcomes Satan himself, and all the bondage he has produced, to regenerate the dead sinner, doesn't he? Can't he, therefore, break through the clinging fog of doubt which is so prevalent in many circles today? Yes, of course he can. Why, then, should any believer doubt his salvation? Why doesn't the Spirit witness with his spirit, and give him that assurance? Indeed, doesn't the Scripture say that the Spirit *does* witness to the believer, *does* anoint and seal him? So why, I ask again, should any believer doubt?

I do not find it easy to answer these questions. Except in this way: the same argument could be used on more than assurance. Take the law. As I have said, the New Testament teaches us plainly that when a sinner trusts Christ he dies to the law, is united to Christ, is married to Christ, and in this way – and only in this way – he bears fruit to God; namely, produces a life of sanctification. Indeed, the New Testament teaches that unless a man has died to the law, he cannot be married to Christ, he cannot bear fruit to God (Rom. 7:1-6). How is it, then, that so many believers deny such teaching – many openly asserting the direct opposite; namely, that the believer *is* under the law, the ten commandments, for sanctification? Are these believers not sanctified? Are they not married to Christ? Of course they are – even though they don't understand the teaching of Scripture, even though they deny the very scriptures which teach the doctrine. Despite this gross mistake, they are, nevertheless, sanctified in Christ! But how is such ignorance possible? Why has the Spirit not taught every believer on the law? How is that there are any believers who advocate the law as the perfect rule for the children of God?

I can't answer that. I don't know. But I am not prepared to say that Reformed believers who argue strongly for the law are not sanctified believers. Some might. But I dare not. I prefer to live with the conundrum. I will do all I can to teach such believers a better way, trying to help them get off the treadmill, pointing them to the Scriptures, pointing them to Christ – and yet, all the time, I have to go on living with the unresolved difficulty of how it's all possible.

Take the believer's union with Christ. Isn't this plainly taught in Romans 6? Of course it is! Yet how is it that so many believers remain in ignorance of the great truth – ignorant of an experience that all have – including these very believers – through their trust in Christ? How is it that Lloyd-Jones, when preaching that chapter, had to confess that he had looked in vain in the Congregational hymn-book for hymns on the subject – all the entries in that section speaking in terms of 'fellowship', something quite different to 'union with Christ'. While the phrase 'in Christ'[10] is ubiquitous throughout the New Testament, how is it that the great majority of believers remain sadly ignorant of their status in Christ – with consequent loss of the joy this must bring?

How is it that some Christians argue vehemently against free and sovereign grace (almost picturing God as one who borders on being impotent), and for the freedom of the will of man, yet continue to thank God for converting them, and pray for others to be converted? Why thank God for what they say he couldn't do, and ask him for what they say he can't do? Why not concentrate on what they claim to be the real power behind the throne – the free will of man? I don't know. But it happens! And confusion spells trouble!

Another example of what I am trying to say, and one closer to the matter in hand, may be found in the sorrow brought about by ignorance and misunderstanding over the state of the believing dead, and the return of Christ. This was not unknown in apostolic times (1 Cor. 15:1-58; 1 Thess. 4:13-18). How did Paul get the Thessalonians out of the sorrow brought about by their ignorance over the truth? By instructing them in the gospel, and taking them to Christ: 'Brothers, we do not want you to be ignorant about those who fall asleep, or to grieve like the rest of men, who have no hope. We believe that Jesus...' (1 Thess. 4:13-14). The same, I suggest, goes for assurance by the Spirit. If I may accommodate the apostle's words: 'Brothers, we do not want you to be ignorant about the witness of the Spirit, or to grieve like doubters, who have no assurance. We believe that Jesus gave us his Spirit...'.

---

[10] The GNB translates 'in Christ' as 'in union with Christ'. Excellent!

So, while a lack of assurance *can* indicate a lack of conversion, I am sure that most *unconverted* will have no qualms about their state,[11] whereas genuine believers will think of the possibility of being deceived, and dread it. They know what it is to pray:

Test me, O LORD, and try me, examine my heart and my mind (Ps. 26: 2).
Search me, O God, and know my heart; test me and know my anxious thoughts. See if there is any offensive way in me, and lead me in the way everlasting (Ps. 139:23-24).

In other words, believers who fear that they might not be truly converted are, in truth, giving evidence that they are! Who else but the Spirit could make a sinner so long for Christ, long to be assured, and dreads to think he might be deceived?[12]

In short, the great contemporary source of that cursed doubt suffered by many believers is the near-ubiquitous emphasis on law (in one form or another – the law of Moses, recipe preaching, or conformity to rule), on works, on sanctification and on introspection (overt or incipient). And this stifles the voice and witness of the Spirit. On the reverse side of the coin, the signal lack of preaching and teaching today on the work of the Spirit (and, I am sorry to have to say, to this I have to plead guilty), the absence of reinforced teaching on the Spirit directing believers to Christ, leads many true believers into a miasma of doubt. But this does not mean that such victims – I use the word advisedly – are not true believers.

Consider the Gospel Standard Strict Baptists. I speak of what I know, having had some association with them, both by experience, and by studying their teaching and writing about it. Alas, a believer reared in that denomination will find it almost impossible to come to biblical assurance and express it. The whole atmosphere is against it. Indeed, the air is heavy with the notion that doubt is good and spiritual, and doubt is the only way to be sure of one's safety in Christ! And yet, in my experience, the spirituality of such people

---

[11] Jude spoke of 'men [who] are blemishes at your love feasts, eating with you *without the slightest qualm*' (Jude 12) – and that despite the apostle's warning (1 Cor. 11:27 – 32).
[12] Some unbelievers, I admit, might wish to avoid hell, and that's all. But this, again, will be fed by defective gospel preaching.

often knocks into a cocked hat the 'spirituality' of believers outside their circle! What a puzzle!

The particular form of trouble I am concerned with here – and which I will explore in the following chapter – is legal assurance, that which is brought about by legal preaching as opposed to gospel preaching. This, I contend, is responsible for much of our introspection and lack of assurance. Speaking as an Englishman, centuries of Puritan teaching have penetrated me to such an extent that it is in my genes and DNA.[13]

And in all this, I am thinking not only of overt legal preaching. Sadly, there is a great deal of the incipient variety: preaching rules, regulations, conformity, and not Christ. And this is often coupled with a low, desiccated view of justification by faith.[14] And the incipient, perhaps more than overt, form of legal preaching carries the can for much of our lack of assurance, and our consequent fear and doubt, and loss of joy.

A.W.Pink analysed this lack of assurance:

The assurance of some of God's dear children has been hindered by a defective ministry. They have sat under teaching which was too one-sided, failing to preserve a due balance between the objective and the subjective aspects of the truth. *They have been encouraged to be far more occupied with self than with Christ.* Knowing that many are deceived, fearful lest they also should be, their main efforts are directed to self-examination. Disgusted, too, by the loud boastings of empty professors, perceiving the worthlessness of the carnal confidence voiced by the frothy religionists all around them, they hesitate to avow the assurance of salvation lest they be guilty of presumption or be puffed up by the devil. Indeed, they have come to regard doubtings, fears and uncertainty, as the best evidence of spiritual humility.[15]

---

[13] Take the sabbath. My father was not a believer, but in the 40s and 50s he would not allow me to play in the street on Sunday (which, because of Puritan teaching, was thought to be the sabbath), my mother would never dream of hanging washing (laundry) on the line, and we had clothes known as 'Sunday best'. 'Better the day, better the deed' was the general catch-phrase to cover any misdemeanour.

[14] See my *Four*.

[15] Pink, emphasis mine.

While I acknowledge that Pink would *not* agree with me as to the 'defective ministry' in question, he has surely put his finger on the spot. It's time we took a hard look at legal teaching on assurance – that which is responsible for the widespread lack of joy among believers today.

Legal Assurance

The New Testament, it is clear, does not describe the believer as a 'wretched man', but speaks of him as one who has ever-increasing glory, liberty and assurance. And this, of course, should be the lot of every believer today. Many Reformed disagree. They think that Romans 7:14-25 represents the believer at his most spiritual, and that most believers never get full assurance; some even think that most believers don't deserve it! They also argue vehemently that the believer is under the law of Moses (usually whittled down, without the slightest justification, to the ten commandments) for sanctification. It's my contention that all this is connected, and explains why so many believers, reared under such a legal system, find themselves in bondage, fear and doubt, often for years, if not decades, if not all their lives. Indeed, many Reformed men preach, teach and write in ways which positively encourage doubt and introspection, fear and lack of assurance. Some even glory in the fact that they make believers anxious! And it's not only where the law is openly and statedly preached. The teaching of legal assurance – or that which leads to it – casts its shadow far wider than that.

Let me set out what I am talking about.[1]

In summary, through his over-reaction to Rome,[2] Calvin went too far in making assurance the essence of faith. Assurance is the

---

[1] Although I will talk about 'the Reformed', clearly not all Reformed teachers take the same line throughout. Some do not go along with the Confessions they talk so highly of, so I am able to quote them speaking scripturally on this issue.

[2] Rome denies even the possibility of assurance: 'No one can know with a certainty of faith... that he has obtained the grace of God' ('The Council of Trent' (documentacatholicaomnia.eu). 'If anyone says that man is absolved from his sins and justified because he firmly believes that he is absolved and justified, or that no one is truly justified except him who believes himself justified... let him be anathema'. 'If anyone says that a man who is born again and justified is bound *ex fide* to believe that he is certainly in the number of the predestined, let him be anathema'. 'If anyone says that he will for certain, with an absolute and infallible

concomitant of faith, not its essence.[3] In so doing, however, he avoided the disastrous consequences which his later-Puritan followers produced. Whether or not in the process he crushed any broken reeds or snuffed out any smoking flax eternity will declare.

Moving on to the Puritans: while the early Puritans largely followed Calvin closely on assurance, the overwhelming majority of later Puritans did not. In one respect – assurance being the essence of faith – they were right, but in making sanctification the way of assurance they were wrong. The consequences of this mistake have been heavy indeed. They are with us to this day, bringing fear and doubt to so many,[4] since far more people are influenced by the late-Puritan view of assurance than they realise.[5] Indeed, some, who would be horrified to be thought Puritan, nevertheless, *are* late-Puritan on assurance (or rather the lack of it) – without an inkling that it is so. Hearing the howls of disbelief, let me make good my case.

I begin with the New England antinomian crisis (1636-1637), the main players being, on the one side, Thomas Hooker and Thomas Shepard, and, on the other, Anne Hutchinson and John Wheelwright. John Cotton tried to steer a middle path between the two – and got away with it, but only by the skin of his teeth – while Henry Vane the Younger, who also played his part, decided to sail back across the Atlantic to England. The story is far more complicated than I can explore here, but in essence Hooker and

---

certainty, have that great gift of perseverance even to the end, unless he shall have learned this by a special revelation, let him be anathema' (canons 14-16) (ewtn.com).

[3] See Appendix 1. Calvin's over-reaction parallels the way his detestation of the Anabaptists blinded him, and drove him even further into infant baptism. See my *Infant*.

[4] Take full account of Beeke's subtitle: *The **Legacy** of **Calvin** and **His** **Successors**!*

[5] It is invidious to give examples – they are legion! – but here are a few. Charles Hodge: *A Commentary on the Second Epistle to the Corinthians*, The Banner of Truth Trust, London, 1963, pp305-306; Robert L.Dabney: *Discussions: Evangelical and Theological*, The Banner of Truth Trust, Edinburgh, 1967, Vol.1 pp214-228; *Systematic Theology*, The Banner of Truth Trust, Edinburgh, 1985, pp611,698-713.

Shepard heavily emphasised the law in preparing the sinner for Christ and in sanctifying the saint, and urged tests of sanctification (and therefore, of course, the work of the law) for assurance. Hutchinson and Wheelwright stoutly resisted this, stressing the freeness of grace in Christ in conversion and sanctification, and the inner witness of the Spirit for assurance.[6] For their pains, they were banished. This controversy spilled over into Old England.

Back in England, the Particular Baptist, William Kiffin, came into doubt through reading Hooker's *The Soul's Preparation for Christ* – a Puritan classic on preparationism, the necessity of preaching the law to prepare sinners for Christ. Kiffin was helped out of his grief by the preaching of John (not to be confused with Thomas) Goodwin who showed him that legal preparationism was wrong. Indeed, Goodwin's preaching, as John Coffey said:

Contrasted sharply with the bleak emphasis on legal preparation... and self-scrutiny that echoed from some Puritan pulpits... His was a message designed to calm the tortured souls who sought counsel from Calvinist pastors.[7]

And so to the Westminster Assembly and its documents – documents which have exerted enormous influence down the centuries, and do so to this very day, some putting them almost on a par with (if not exceeding) the Bible itself! The Westminster documents, as I have noted, are heavy on law. This is no surprise since one of the main purposes in setting up the Assembly was to deal with antinomianism (both real and imagined) in England. The

---

[6] Sadly, Cotton believed in eternal justification (Bauckham p45). For the arguments against this hyper-Calvinistic error, see my *Eternal*. But on assurance, Cotton was right. He argued that 'the first, the primary evidence of regeneration [is] not any aspect of sanctification but purely the witness of the Spirit in the heart of the regenerate man... Cotton... held that the primary evidence was the witness of the Spirit enabling a man to receive and hold in faith the unconditional promise of God's free grace to the elect, that in fact saving faith itself was the first and sufficient evidence of regeneration' (Bauckham p45). See Hall *passim*. Remember all this was played out in 'the antinomian crisis' raging at the time.
[7] Coffey pp52-54. Incidentally, many praise the Puritans as fine physicians of the soul. No doubt they were, but not a few of their patients were diseased though their physicians' own teaching!

solution it came up with was to put Calvin's law system into full effect. And how!

Now listen to the Westminster Confession on assurance. Take first, assurance as to the Bible being the word of God:

> Our full persuasion and assurance of the infallible truth and divine authority thereof, is from the inward work of the Holy Spirit bearing witness by and with the word in our hearts.[8]

Excellent! But what about assurance of salvation?

> This certainty is not a bare conjectural and probable persuasion grounded upon a fallible hope; but an infallible assurance of faith founded upon the divine truth of the promises of salvation, the inward evidence of those graces unto which these promises are made, the testimony of the Spirit of adoption witnessing with our spirits that we are the children of God, which Spirit is the earnest of our inheritance, whereby we are sealed to the day of redemption.[9]

And then, for our purposes, the punch line:

> This infallible assurance does not so belong to the essence of faith, but that a true believer may wait long, and conflict with many difficulties, before he be partaker of it.

While I agree that assurance is not the essence, but a concomitant, of faith,[10] it is how the Westminster statement goes on that makes for trouble. Proof texts offered to establish this struggle for assurance are 1 John 5:13; Isaiah 1:10; Mark 9:24; and Psalms 77 and 88. Whether or not those texts really do establish the Assembly's assertions, reader, I leave for you to decide. I know what I think!

Here is a clear parting of the ways with Calvin; in fact, Westminster flatly contradicts the Reformer.[11] What is more, the believer who takes Westminster as definitive *can* be assured, but he may have to wait long for it, and the path to it may be fraught with difficulties. Indeed, he must be prepared never to get it! And

---

[8] 1 John 2:20,27; John 16:13-14; 1 Cor. 2:10-12; Isa. 59:21.
[9] Heb. 6:11,17-9; 2 Pet. 1:4-5,10-11; 1 John 2:3; 3:14; 2 Cor. 1:12,21-22; Rom. 8:15-16; Eph.1:13-14; 4:30.
[10] See Appendix 1.
[11] Despite the reconciliation attempted by some – see Chrisco.

remember, reader, that millions of believers have taken, and many still do take, the Westminster as authoritative. Millions, therefore, are on the high road to lack of assurance before they start. Since 'they drank in Puritan divinity with their mothers' milk',[12] no wonder they grew up with the consequences. Feed a child on the wrong diet, and the effects may well be permanent. As for Timothy, we know that, under the tutelage of his mother and grandmother, he had been reared on a diet of Scripture, and this led him to salvation (2 Tim. 1:5; 3:14-17). Is it beyond the realms of possibility to think that somebody reared, from pre-conversion days, on a diet of law, assurance by sanctification and assurance an experience only for the elite, might present symptoms of fear and doubt? The same may be said, of course, of those who are under the 1689 Particular Baptist Confession, one which is almost identical to the Westminster.

John Owen (a man of the Savoy Declaration which depended heavily on the Westminster Confession) went even further than Westminster. Believer, if you want to be kept awake at nights, read Owen on assurance just before you switch out the light! Hear him:

Very few on gospel grounds do attain to [assurance]... It is a great and rare thing to have forgiveness in God discovered [made known] unto a sinful soul.

Owen spoke of someone who testified to twenty years' struggle with 'trials, difficulties, temptations, [he had] wrestled with... before [he eventually] obtained it'. Owen: 'It is the duty of every believer to labour after an assurance of a personal interest in forgiveness'. Clearly, however, he must not expect it to come easily, if at all, since it is rarely attained. Owen himself struggled with it for five years.[13] He offered three main reasons for this

---

[12] Calvin on 2 Tim. 1:5, speaking of Timothy: 'He had been educated from his infancy in such a manner that he might have sucked godliness along with his milk'.

[13] Owen pp386,413-414,431,508-509, emphasis mine. In his earlier works – two catechisms – Owen had thought of assurance as an integral part of faith. Beeke surmised as to the reason for his change of view. Was it the Westminster documents or his own experience coupled with that of the people to whom he preached? (Beeke: *Quest* p166). Either, it seems to me,

difficulty: 'The constant voice of conscience lies against it'; 'the law lies against this discovery'; 'inbred notions that are in the heart of man about God's holiness and vindictive justice' lie against it.[14] Don't miss number two!

Thomas Brooks was another Puritan to put a grim prospect before his readers:

Now though this full assurance is earnestly desired, and highly prized, and the want of it much lamented, and the enjoyment of it much endeavoured after by all saints, *yet it is only obtained by a few*. Assurance is a mercy too good for most men's hearts, it is a crown too weighty for most men's heads. Assurance is *optimum maximum*, the best and greatest mercy; and therefore God will only give it to his best and dearest friends... Assurance is that 'tried gold' (Rev. 3:18)... God only gives to tried friends. Among those few that have a share or portion in the special love and favour of God, there are but a very few that have an assurance of his love. It is one mercy for God to love the soul, and another mercy for God to assure the soul of his love.[15]

Not much hope here, then! Hardly any at all! Heaven on earth? Maybe – but only for the few. I wonder where Brooks found the scriptural warrant for telling believers that 'assurance... [is] only obtained by a few... [it being] too good for most' believers. Indeed, I ask myself why Brooks wrote his book – a book describing a wonderful experience for believers, but one which the majority of them will never get, even after a life-time of desperate searching for it, since they are not good enough for it! It would seem tantamount to cruelty on Brooks' part, taunting the overwhelming majority of believers with the golden apple always just out of reach! I wonder why such a book is thought to be worthy of publication today – unless, of course, it is to bolster the Reformed emphasis on law. Do the publishers *want* believers to be miserable? Hardly a recommendation for their law system, is it?

Richard Baxter:

For those doubts of my own salvation, which exercised me many years, the chiefest causes of them were these... because I could not

---

gives the game away! We must be men of Scripture before men of Confession or experience.

[14] Owen pp387,389,431, emphasis mine.

[15] Brooks p335, emphasis mine.

distinctly trace the workings of the Spirit upon my heart *in that method which Mr Bolton, Mr Hooker, Mr Rogers, and other divines describe...* I was once [inclined] to meditate on my own heart... I was continually poring either on my sins or wants, or examining my sincerity. [16]

A hundred years later, Jonathan Edwards trod the same path. At one stage, he doubted his 'interest in God's love and favour... because', he said, 'I cannot speak so fully to my experience of that preparatory work, *of which the divines speak...* [and] I do not remember that I experienced regeneration, *exactly in those steps*, in which divines say it is generally wrought'. Later, he felt some relief concerning his 'trust and affiance in Christ, and with delight committing of my soul to him, *of which our divines used to speak*, and about which I have been somewhat in doubt'. Yet, later again, he still had to wonder: 'Whether I am now converted or not'. Even so, he vowed to use 'for helps *some of our old divines*'.[17] In other words, Edwards was in a hole and proceeded to dig deeper, using the same tools as got him into the hole in the first place!

Asahel Nettleton, a man greatly used of God in the Second Great Awakening in New England, was 'exceedingly cautious in speaking about his belief that he was accepted of God'. So much so, he had a very low opinion of his standing before God: 'The most that I have ventured to say respecting myself is that I think it possible I may get to heaven'.[18]

Then we have John Newton:

'Tis a point I long to know,
Oft it causes anxious thought;
Do I love the Lord, or no?
Am I his, or am I not?

If I love, why am I thus?
Why this dull and lifeless frame?
Hardly, sure, can they be worse,
Who have never heard his name!

---

[16] Baxter pp10,113, emphasis mine.
[17] Edwards: *Diary* xxiv,xxxv,xxxvi, emphasis mine.
[18] Tyler and Bonar p30.

Could my heart so hard remain,
Prayer a task and burden prove;
Every trifle give me pain,
If I knew a Saviour's love?

When I turn my eyes within,
All is dark, and vain, and wild;
Filled with unbelief and sin,
Can I deem myself a child?

If I pray, or hear, or read,
Sin is mixed with all I do;
You that love the Lord indeed,
Tell me: Is it thus with you?

Yet I mourn my stubborn will,
Find my sin a grief and thrall;
Should I grieve for what I feel,
If I did not love at all?

Could I joy his saints to meet,
Choose the ways I once abhorred,
Find, at times, the promise sweet,
If I did not love the Lord?

Lord, decide the doubtful case!
Thou who art thy people's Sun;
Shine upon thy work of grace,
If it be indeed begun.

Let me love thee more and more,
If I love at all, I pray;
If I have not loved before,
Help me to begin today.

Yes, Newton got some sort of relief, and some measure of assurance, but hardly a ringing endorsement of the biblical position, is it?

Lloyd-Jones thought that 'many Christian people have only known this [sealing, assurance] just before their death'.[19]

James Sawyer: 'In San Diego in November, 1989, at the Evangelical Theological Society annual meeting, Dr John MacArthur was asked when a believer could be assured of his

---

[19] Lloyd-Jones: *God's* p299.

salvation; his reply was that such assurance could be had only after death'.[20] There is an element of truth in this, of course, but as it stands it surely misrepresents the New Testament.

I need not labour the point. Do not miss the full implications of the title Beeke chose for his large volume on the subject: *The **Quest** for Full Assurance*. Reader, if you seek assurance by the Reformed route, you must prepare yourself for a long and arduous search, one which, in all probability, will be in vain. Gird your loins up, grit your teeth: months, maybe years, of nail-biting – if not white-knuckled – doubt and fear lie ahead! If I may accommodate the words of Brutus (according to William Shakespeare): 'All the voyage of [your] life is [almost certain to be] bound in shallows and in miseries'.

We don't need further evidence from Confessions, sermons and books. Too many believers can read the signs of this anxiety all too clearly in their own hearts, even though they may not realise where it has all come from. Those locked in this system know only too well that they are in trouble. Many may just be resigned to a life of doubt. Some may even regard their doubt as a mark of the highest spirituality – and so get some kind of relief that way!

Some saints cannot even face it. One Lord's day morning, I had just started to preach a sermon on Romans 8:33-34, when a lady (a believer, married to a full-time gospel worker) got up and left the meeting. After the service, the local leaders assured me that this was not unexpected since (unknown to me) the lady had long wrestled with lack of assurance. Alas! If only she had remained! She might have been helped – even brought out of her condition. Walking out of a sermon on such a passage was the last thing she should have done.[21]

This case is far from isolated. I know that many believers are in bondage and fear. Liberty and joy ought to be the lot of believers (2 Cor. 3:17-18; Gal. 5:1,13; 1 Pet. 1:8, for instance), but too often, it

---

[20] Sawyer (bible.org).

[21] For a short address on the passage, see my 'Christ, Not Law, Banishes Fear' (David H J Gay Ministry sermonaudio.com). It may also be found as a chapter in my *Grace*.

is not. Hence my book. I hope that what I write here might help some impoverished believers break free of their desperate plight.

What is the thinking behind all this legal assurance?

The doctrine undergirding legal assurance
The common view of assurance today – if it's thought about at all! – has three steps or levels, each rising in importance. *First*, the believer rests himself upon the bare word of God. The Scriptures promise that if I believe I shall be saved (Acts 16:31); I do believe; therefore I am saved.[22] *Secondly*, the believer tests his life by various evidences spelled out in Scripture – in 1 John, for instance. I love the brothers; therefore, I must be saved (1 John 3:14). And, *thirdly*, there is the direct evidence of the inner witness of the Spirit (Rom. 8:16), the sealing of the Spirit (2 Cor. 1:22; Eph. 1:13-14; 4:30), the 'anointing' (2 Cor. 1:21-22; 1 John 2:20,27). 'He who believes in the Son of God has the witness in himself' (1 John 5:10). And we have the repeated experience of 'being filled with the Spirit' (Luke 1:15,41,67; 4:1; Acts 2:4; 4:8,31; 6:3,5; 9:17; 11:24; 13:52; Eph. 5:18).

This, I say, is the way most Reformed (evangelical) teachers today speak of assurance – defining it in these three steps, *and in this order*. And they usually place the third step beyond the reach of most believers.[23] Let me prove it.

Take Lloyd-Jones:

---

[22] As I have shown, modern Sandemanians often stop here.

[23] I am glad to record that Erroll Hulse, for one, questioned it. 'A well-grounded assurance is based firstly on the inward witness of the Holy Spirit testifying to sonship. Secondly, and no less essentially, it is based on a spiritual life which is in harmony with sonship, not one or the other, but both together' (Hulse: Believer's p121). I would nuance this by changing Hulse's second 'based' to 'verified' – especially with regard to others, since a sanctified life is the only way one can be assured about another person. I will come back to this. Again, Hulse had to struggle to get to this position seeing he had started so badly in his chapter: 'No Genuine Experience Without the Law' (Hulse pp67-70). Iain H.Murray steered a middle course through the Reformed minefield, while trying hard to defend the standard position (Iain H.Murray pp167-200. He, too, advocated preaching the law to sinners, and to saints for their sanctification (Iain H.Murray pp8-15,23-37,47-54,64,69,91).

This [that is, the inner witness] is the highest form of assurance possible; there is nothing beyond it. It is the acme, the zenith of assurance and certainty of salvation!

Lloyd-Jones started with the first level:

There is a form of assurance which is derived from deduction from the Scriptures. That is the form of assurance which most Christians seem to have, and many believe it is the only form of assurance.

Lloyd-Jones moved on to the second form of assurance; namely the tests of 1 John:

That takes you a step further than the first one; it is better than the first one. The first was merely believing the bare word of God [Sandemanianism!], but now you have examined your life and you are sure that you are not merely saying these things in a theoretical or intellectual manner; you are really living them.[24]

And then he reached the peak:

But there is a third step... [Rom. 8:16]. This is entirely the action of the Holy Spirit himself. I do nothing about it; it is entirely 'given'. It is solely and exclusively what he does to me... It is the Spirit himself who does it. We do no deducing here. It is not the result of syllogism [deduction], or of argumentation. It is the Spirit himself doing it to me... This testimony of the Spirit with our spirit [is] this highest possible form of assurance.[25]

This is typical of the teaching of many today. But what is the biblical ground for this order? None! None whatever! It is pure invention, a template imposed on Scripture. Oh! Many say it (and peer repetition is bewitching – teacher repetition, even more so), but what *scriptural* proof do they offer? As I showed, the New Testament speaks often and repeatedly of every believer having the Spirit and, therefore, having assurance – and all without having to go through the drawn-out process of introspection, probing one's sanctification.

---

[24] I expose the wrongness of this in Appendix 3.
[25] Lloyd-Jones: *Sons* pp302-305,309. See also Lloyd-Jones: 'Sandemanianism' pp187-188; *God's* pp262-263. Oddly – since he was so strong against Sandemanianism – Lloyd-Jones, of all people, did not seem to see the connection between the above and Sandemanianism.

Take just one example: Romans 8. Nobody can question that this chapter speaks of the believer's assurance; notice, the *believer's* assurance, not the apostle's or that of some favoured few. How did the early believers get this assurance? Those at Rome had it long before this chapter, of course, but Paul surely put his finger on it when he declared:

If anyone does not have the Spirit of Christ, he does not belong to Christ... Those who are led by the Spirit of God are sons of God. For you [believers, all of you] did not receive a spirit that makes you a slave again to fear, but you received the Spirit of sonship. And by him we cry: 'Abba, Father'. The Spirit himself testifies with our spirit that we are God's children. Now if we are children, then we are heirs – heirs of God and co-heirs with Christ, if indeed we share in his sufferings in order that we may also share in his glory (Rom. 8:9,14-17).

We have, of course, covered this ground already, but my point here is this: Where, in Romans, did Paul put any tests to believers so that they might obtain assurance? That is, where in the letter to the Romans, did Paul urge the believers to look at their works to see if they were really converted? Nowhere! There is not a single test for assurance in the entire book of Romans. Is there one in Ephesians? In Thessalonians?

Take that last. There is a place for assurance by works. Oh? Yes! Paul was assured of the Thessalonian believers' election (1 Thess. 1:4), he was convinced of it. How? By the effect the gospel had in their lives; in other words, the apostle argued their election from the evidence of their conversion and sanctification. There is no other way, of course. The Spirit never bears witness with our spirit that someone else is a child of God!

Calvin, commenting on Philippians 1:6:

It is asked, however, whether anyone can be certain as to the salvation of others, for Paul here is not speaking of himself but of the Philippians. I answer, that the assurance which an individual has respecting his own salvation, is very different from what he has as to that of another. For the Spirit of God is a witness to me of my calling, as he is to each of the elect. As to others, we have no testimony, except from the outward efficacy of the Spirit; that is, in so far as the grace of God shows itself in them, so that we come to know it. There is, therefore, a great difference, because the assurance of faith remains inwardly shut up, and does not extend itself to others. But wherever we see any such tokens of divine election as can be perceived by us, we ought immediately to be stirred up to entertain good hope.

But this is not the real question! Where are we told that the Thessalonians got *their own* assurance by probing their sanctification? Where do we read of them being commanded to search *their* works to discover if *they* were true believers?

Moving on to the 'sealing of the Spirit', Lloyd-Jones was unequivocal. He defined 'sealing' as 'authenticity and authority, ownership, and security and safety'.[26] 'It means that we can be authenticated, that it can be established by intelligible signs that we are indeed the children of God, heirs of God, and joint-heirs with our blessed Lord and Saviour Jesus Christ';[27] in a word, assured. But do not miss the 'can'. Much grief lies buried in that small word. He went on: While 'you cannot be a Christian without receiving the Holy Spirit', nevertheless 'one can be a Christian without the sealing of the Spirit'. And though he admitted that he was flying in the face of 'the prevailing common teaching',[28] Lloyd-Jones was adamant that he was right. One of his arguments (in addition to the support of some Puritans!) was that the translators of the AV 'deliberately introduced' – his words – the word 'after' in Ephesians 1:13,[29] showing that they were convinced sealing was a later experience, after conversion. 'Are we to seek this sealing? My answer, without any hesitation', said Lloyd-Jones, 'is that we should most certainly do so'. But, he warned, this is no easy task or one which is quickly over: 'Prepare the way... mortify... cleanse yourselves... put into practice the virtues... labour at it... pray for this blessing... be desperate for it'. Alas, however, according to Lloyd-Jones, 'many Christian people have only known this [sealing, assurance] just before their death'.[30]

But where are we told this in the New Testament? Where are we told of any New Testament believer who was seeking assurance,

---

[26] Lloyd- Jones: *God's* p245.

[27] Lloyd- Jones: *God's* p248.

[28] I am not so sure – if you include the huge number of believers who never even think about it, and are never taught about it!

[29] Quite wrong, as I have explained.

[30] Lloyd-Jones: *God's* pp248-249,266,294-300.

the witness, sealing or anointing of the Spirit? Where are we told that it is the duty of believers to discover if they are converted and so be assured? In Puritan literature, we find plenty, but where in Scripture?[31]

When preaching through Romans, on reaching Romans 8:15 Lloyd-Jones made a dramatic switch in his application of the apostle's words. Notice how, from, say, verse 9 to verse 14, Paul speaks in terms of 'you' and 'we'. Clearly, he is speaking to and of all believers – as Lloyd-Jones agreed, by applying the words to all believers. Suddenly, however, Lloyd-Jones switched, and started restricting the apostle's 'you' to some special believers:

The 'Spirit of adoption' is not essential to salvation, for a person can be a Christian and yet know little or nothing about this Spirit of adoption.[32]

---

[31] Despite the extract from Spurgeon which I placed at the start of my book, I do not see this in Ps. 35:1-3: 'O LORD... say to my soul: "I am your salvation"'. David was praying for reassurance in face of bitter attack, even though he had this assurance (Ps. 62:2). In any case, neither verse is in the New Testament, and we are speaking about assurance in the new covenant.

[32] Lloyd-Jones: *Sons* p246. Lloyd-Jones admitted he had 'the majority of the... Reformers... Luther and Calvin in particular' against him. In what followed, to justify his claim, Lloyd-Jones offered the Westminster Confession, but no scripture. A significant part of *Sons* is taken up with historical lectures rather than preaching. Again: 'The Reformers were... men who believed in possessing assurance of salvation... Do you believe in assurance of salvation as the Protestant Reformers did?... Those Protestant Reformers said that a man is not truly saved unless he had assurance!... Whenever the church is powerful and mighty and authoritative, her preachers and ministers have always been men who speak out of the full assurance of faith, and know in whom they have believed. It was for this reason that the martyrs could smile... and go gladly to the stake; they knew that from the stake they would wake in heaven and glory and see him [Christ] face to face! And they rejoiced in the assurance of salvation!' (D.Martyn Lloyd-Jones: *Knowing The Times...*, The Banner Of Truth Trust, Edinburgh, 1989, pp100-101. Even so, Lloyd-Jones still ploughed on. Incidentally, once again he let the cat out of the bag: his view on assurance was not governed by Scripture but by experience.

Lloyd-Jones supported his mistaken interpretation of Romans 8:15 by pointing out that if it is true that every believer has the witness of the Spirit, then it follows that professing believers who do not have that witness cannot be converted. And this, of course, could shatter *true* believers. He deduced, therefore, that not every believer has the witness of the Spirit.[33]

In reply, I say four things. *First*, Lloyd-Jones was making the bad mistake of allowing experience (if not feelings) govern his interpretation of Scripture. *Secondly*, Lloyd-Jones may well have been right about some professors. Professors can be unbelievers – witness his own and his wife's testimony.[34] *Thirdly*, as I have been careful to explain, true believers can lose their assurance. Just as in Galatians and 1 John, men can be taken into spiritual bondage through wrong teaching, so here; the legal teachers themselves have produced the lack of assurance by their law teaching! A lack of assurance, therefore, does not necessarily indicate an unconverted state. Moreover, there is such a thing as false assurance. And that takes me to the *fourth* thing I want to say by way of reply to Lloyd-Jones. The obverse of his position can only mean that all who say they are assured must be truly converted. But the unregenerate can be quite secure, and there is always the Sandemanian problem! To sum up: we must always start with Scripture, and fix on that, before we turn to experience, feelings or logic.

Getting back to Ephesians, having left the road on 'the sealing of the Spirit' (Eph. 1:13-14), it's no wonder that Lloyd-Jones went even further astray as he moved on to the following verses (Eph. 1:15-23), and asked this question: 'What is it that [the apostle] has in mind'? Listen to Lloyd-Jones' answer! He immediately plunged into 'tests':

[Paul]... supplies us with tests which we can [he really meant 'must'] apply to ourselves. How do we know we are Christians?[35]... What are our grounds for thanking God that we are Christians... The mere fact that we think we are Christians is not enough[36]... There must be some

---

[33] Lloyd-Jones: *Sons* pp246-247.

[34] See my *Infant*.

[35] I agree with the next sentence: 'How can others know we are Christians?'

[36] No – but the witness and sealing of the Spirit is no 'mere fact'.

test. It we are to have real and solid assurance, then we must have some valid tests to apply; and fortunately for us the apostle provides them for us here.[37]

He does not! Paul tells the Ephesians that he is praying for them that they might enjoy all that they have in Christ! Lloyd-Jones was doing what so many do today; he was turning the gospel into law! Let Paul speak for himself. See, reader, if you think Paul was setting out a series of tests by which the believer should measure himself in order to get assurance:

You... were included in Christ when you heard the word of truth, the gospel of your salvation. Having believed, you were marked in him with a seal, the promised Holy Spirit, who is a deposit guaranteeing our inheritance until the redemption of those who are God's possession – to the praise of his glory. For this reason, ever since I heard about your faith in the Lord Jesus and your love for all the saints, I have not stopped giving thanks for you, remembering you in my prayers. I keep asking that the God of our Lord Jesus Christ, the glorious Father, may give you the Spirit of wisdom and revelation, so that you may know him better. I pray also that the eyes of your heart may be enlightened in order that you may know the hope to which he has called you, the riches of his glorious inheritance in the saints, and his incomparably great power for us who believe. That power is like the working of his mighty strength, which he exerted in Christ when he raised him from the dead and seated him at his right hand in the heavenly realms, far above all rule and authority, power and dominion, and every title that can be given, not only in the present age but also in the one to come. And God placed all things under his feet and appointed him to be head over everything for the church, which is his body, the fullness of him who fills everything in every way (Eph. 1:13-23).

I fail to see that Paul was here setting out tests whereby believers could and should search themselves as to the reality of their experience.[38]

John Stott, referring to Lloyd-Jones' exposition of these verses – that it is a special experience reserved for just the elite – rightly stated of that interpretation and assertion:

---

[37] Lloyd-Jones: *God's* p314.
[38] See my short address on the passage: 'Trinitarian Experience' (David H J Gay Ministry sermonaudio.com).

My anxiety is whether the biblical texts have been rightly interpreted. I have the uneasy feeling that it is the experiences which have determined the exposition. For the natural reading of Romans 8:14-17 is surely that *all* believers are 'led by the Spirit' (Rom. 8:14), have 'received a [the] Spirit of adoption' (Rom. 8:15), and cry 'Abba, Father' as the Spirit himself bears witness to them that they are God's children (Rom. 8:16) and therefore also his heirs (Rom. 8:17). There is no indication in these four verses that a special, distinctive or overwhelming experience is in mind which needs to be sought by all though it is given only to some. On the contrary, the whole paragraph appears to be descriptive of what is, or should be, common to all believers. Though doubtless in differing degrees of intensity, all who have the Spirit's indwelling (Rom. 8:9) are given the Spirit's witness too (Rom. 8:15-16).[39]

Excellent, though I would strengthen Stott's words. I am sure that Lloyd-Jones did allow experience to govern exposition. Indeed, he said so – pointing out that the 'natural reading' means that those who don't receive such a witness are not true believers. Again, I would stiffen Stott's use of 'appears' in the following: 'The whole paragraph appears to be descriptive of what is... common to all believers'.[40] It is – in the New Testament!

And now for Jonathan Edwards. I have already quoted him grieving over his doubt. As you may well imagine, he had the doctrinal thinking behind his lack of assurance well and truly worked out. But just listen to it! Let Edwards' words sink in! As his editors noted, Edwards, in his sermon: 'I Know That My Redeemer Lives', which he preached in October 1740, showed he had departed from George Whitefield[41] on assurance: 'Edwards

---

[39] Stott p236, emphasis his. Referring to Lloyd-Jones' heavy dependence on the testimony of those who claimed to have remarkable experiences, Hulse rightly spoke of Lloyd-Jones' 'story-telling rather than exposition' (*Reformation*, no.84, 1985, p13, in Atherstone and Jones pp123-130).

[40] Notice my omission of 'or should be'.

[41] See the earlier note on Whitefield's letter to John Wesley. What about the Welsh Calvinistic Methodists with whom Whitefield was closely associated? Howell Harris, though he lost his sense of assurance for a while, as Evans noted, 'was adamant that assurance was the essence of saving faith'. This was a mistake – see Appendix 1. He asked Whitefield to write on the subject, promising to translate the work into Welsh. 'It is much wanting', he told him. But Whitefield didn't comply. William

emphasises that it is only through long-term manifestation and practice of "holy fruits" that the believer can achieve assurance – but never any absolute certainty – of salvation'. As he himself declared: 'Another thing that is requisite to assurance is frequent and strict self-examination... Christians should be often examining themselves'.[42]

Six years later, Edwards wrote his *Religious Affections*, in which he spoke about 'the witness of the Spirit':

That which many call the witness of the Spirit, is no other than an immediate suggestion and impression of that fact, otherwise secret, that they are made the children of God, and so that their sins are pardoned, and that God has given them a title to heaven.

Do not misread Edwards here: he was being utterly dismissive! Referring to his grandfather, Solomon Stoddard, Edwards was pleased to say that though in his younger days Stoddard had believed the above, latterly he had come to see that 'the Spirit discovers [reveals] the grace of God in Christ, and thereby draws forth special actings of faith and love, which are evidential; but it does not work by way of testimony'. Edwards, analysing the 'error', argued that it missed the essential point; namely, *evidence*. In the following, I highlight the relevant words – and glosses:

Williams translated Ralph Erskine's *The Assurance of Faith*. In the societies, the first question was: 'Do you know that you believe?' Evans: 'It is clear that the Welsh Methodists were being taught that assurance was the Christian's birthright'. Although Harris and Daniel Rowland had some disagreement over the matter, in a sermon reported by Harris, Rowland 'showed that all the saints had a witness... and that all [might] doubt for a time, but don't abide in it. It is a mark of the hypocrite to be easy without testimony'. An anonymous critic noted that Rowland and Whitefield agreed on 'election... regeneration.. and personal assurance of salvation'. Evans observed that the 1742 rules showed that their 'hallmark was, unashamedly, assurance of salvation' (Evans pp89,111-115,12,146,157,184-185,191,252-253). Lloyd-Jones on Harris' conversion, quoting Harris himself: 'I know my sins have been forgiven', went on: 'Howell Harris was now converted, he knows that his sins are forgiven, and he has lost his burden' (Lloyd-Jones 'Howell' p285.

[42] Kimnach, Minkema and Sweeney xxxii, p160.

When God sets his seal on a man's heart by his Spirit, there is some holy stamp, some image impressed, and left upon the heart by the Spirit, as by the seal upon the wax. And this holy stamp, or impressed image, exhibiting clear *evidence* to the conscience, that the subject of it is the child of God, is the very thing which in Scripture is called 'the seal of the Spirit', and 'the witness' or '*evidence* of the Spirit'. And this mark enstamped by the Spirit on God's children, is his own image. That is the *evidence* by which they are known to be God's children.

This is vital. Edwards has radically shifted the biblical position – the direct witness of the Spirit – to assurance based on evidence; namely, sanctification. He did this by 'correcting' Paul! The apostle said 'witness'; Edwards said 'evidence'. The plain fact is a witness *gives* evidence; it is not *the* evidence! Edwards made his tampering with Paul abundantly plain in his comments on Romans 8:16:

When [the apostle] speaks of the Spirit giving us 'witness' or *evidence* that we are God's children, [he is referring to the Spirit's] dwelling in us, and leading us, as a spirit of adoption, or of a child, disposing us to behave towards God as a father... So that the witness of the Spirit... is far from being any whisper, or immediate suggestion; but is that gracious, holy *effect* of the Spirit of God in the hearts of saints, the disposition and temper [spirit, attitude, frame of mind] of children, appearing in sweet child-like love to God, which casts out fear. It is plain that the apostle speaks of the Spirit... as dwelling in the hearts of saints, as a gracious principle, in opposition to the flesh... It is 'perfect love', or 'strong love' only, which so witnesses or *evidences* that we are children, as to cast out fear, and wholly deliver from the spirit of bondage. The strong and lively *experiences* of evangelical, humble love to God, give clear *evidence* of the soul's relation to God, as his child... The Spirit of God gives the *evidence*, by infusing and shedding abroad the love of God, the spirit of a child, in the heart; and our spirit, or our conscience, receives and declares this *evidence* for our rejoicing. Many mischiefs have arisen from that false and delusive notion of the witness of the Spirit, that it is a kind of inward voice, suggestion, or declaration from God to a man, that he is beloved, pardoned, elected, or the like... It is to be feared that multitudes of souls have been eternally undone by it [ruined by this delusion][43]...The 'witness' or seal of the Spirit consists in the *effect* of the Spirit of God in the heart, in the implantation and *exercises* of grace there, and so consists in *experience*... In these *exercises* of grace in practice, God gives witness,

---

[43] Edwards: *Religious* (New York) p128.

and sets to his seal, in the most conspicuous, eminent, and *evident* manner... And when the apostle speaks of the 'witness' of the Spirit, in Rom. 8:15-17, he has a more immediate respect to what the Christians *experienced* in their *exercises* of love to God, while suffering persecution, as is plain by the context.

Is it? Edwards referred to their 'sufferings' (Rom. 8:18), calling them 'persecutions'. I agree that the apostle moves on to persecutions at the end of the chapter, but it stretches the elastic beyond breaking point to read all that back into 'the witness of the Spirit'. The witness of the Spirit helps believers in their trials and sufferings, but those sufferings, and the believer's attitude under them, are not part of the Spirit's witness.

Edwards tackled those who objected to his teaching on the grounds that it is 'a legal doctrine... [which] magnifies works, and tends to lead men to make too much of their own doings, to the diminution of the glory of free grace'.[44] But so it is, and so it

---

[44] Edwards: *Works* Vol.1 pp1248-1253,1410,1427. See also pp1212,1237-1239,1244,1254,1287,1295,1506,1722,1726; Vol.2 pp97,1041,1229,1234, 2310,2398 (hopefaithprayer.com). Edwards did better, but still did not reach the biblical position, when he wrote: 'Hence we learn, that our experience of the sufficiency of the doctrine of the gospel to give peace of conscience is a rational inward witness to the truth of the gospel. When the mind sees such a fitness in this way of salvation, that it takes off the burden that arises from the sense of its being necessarily bound to punishment... it is a strong argument... not a thing of mere human imagination. When we experience its fitness to answer its end, this is the third of the three that bear witness on earth [1 John 5:6-8]. The Spirit bears witness, by discovering [revealing] the divine glory, and those stamps of divinity that are in the gospel' (Vol.2 p1567). 'The filial Spirit, or Spirit of the Son, or Spirit of adoption, is a principle that, so far as it prevails, excludes and renders the saints incapable of fear, or a legal principle, or spirit of bondage (1 John 4:18)... It is in Christians a principle of love, of childlike confidence and hope... It cries: "Abba, Father". It evidences to them their being the children of God, and begets that trust and assurance that renders them incapable of a legal principle (Rom. 8:15-16)... Being led by the Spirit of the Son of God, as a Spirit of adoption, is inconsistent with a state of bondage, [just] as sonship is inconsistent with servitude: "Where the Spirit of the Lord is, there is liberty" (2 Cor. 3:17)' (Vol.2 p2105). 'Christians are the children of God, as partaking with Christ, the only-begotten Son, in his sonship... And Christians, being the children of God,

does![45] While I agree that justification by faith leads to sanctification in works – of that there is not the slightest doubt – we are talking, as Paul was talking in Romans 8:15-17, about the witness of the Spirit, not the witness of our works. Clearly, Edwards had fundamentally shifted the focus from the biblical position – the witness of the Spirit – to the witness of evidences of life, the witness of works. And this, of course, leads directly to introspection and lack of assurance – as it did, do not forget, in his own experience! Moreover, as I have shown, Edwards called his hearers and readers to frequent self-searching over the matter.

And what a strange childhood he must have had! Evidently he never knew he was the child of his parents until he could see that he really loved them! What is more, how could he have ever fully accepted that he was indeed his father's child – was his love for his father ever 'perfect' (his own word)? There is truth in all he says as regards secondary evidence when faith is tested,[46] and in demonstrating the reality of our profession to others, yes, but as for it being a fair representation of the apostle's words, it is anything but! Try Edwards' treatment on, say, justification by faith in Romans 3 and 4!

Moving on to A.W.Pink: Pink, in part quoting Baxter, was another to call for self-searching for assurance:

A reliable and satisfactory assurance can only be attained or reached by means of a thorough self-examination.[47] 'O therefore, Christians, rest not till you can call this rest your own. Sit not down without assurance. Get alone, and bring your heart to the bar of trial: force it to answer the interrogatories put to it to set the qualifications of the saints on one side, and the qualifications of yourself on the other side, and then judge what resemblance there is between them. You have the same word before you, by which to judge yourself now, as you shall be judged by at the great day. You may there read the very articles upon which you shall be tried; try yourself by these articles now. You may there know beforehand on what terms men shall then be acquitted or condemned.

---

are honoured of God as such. They are sometimes[!] owned as such by the inward testimony of the Spirit of God... "The Spirit bears witness with our spirits that we are the children of God'" (Vol.2 p2311).

[45] See the New England controversy in the previous century.

[46] See Appendix 3.

[47] This denigrates the Spirit's witness to the edge of blasphemy!

Try now whether you are possessed of that which will acquit you, or whether you are in the condition of those that will be condemned; and accordingly acquit or condemn yourself. Yet be sure you judge by a true touchstone, and mistake not the Scripture description of a saint, that you neither acquit nor condemn yourself by mistake'.[48]

Here you have it. Introspection and evidence are the keys to assurance!

John Murray kept to the beaten track; he had *five* 'grounds of assurance': 'An intelligent understanding of the nature of salvation... The recognition of the immutability of the gifts and calling of God... Obedience to the commands of God... Self examination... The inward witness of the Holy Spirit'. Note where Murray placed the witness of the Spirit. Furthermore, he was explicit in placing the other 'grounds' between the believer and his assurance: 'The direct witness of the sonship of believers must never be divorced from the other activities of the Spirit in the sanctification of all believers'. Quite right! But – and what a 'but' – Murray showed where, in his opinion, the weight must fall:

This progressive conformity to the image of God's Son is [the] authentic witness to the recognition that their alignments are not with the world that lies in the wicked one, but with the kingdom which righteousness and peace, and joy in the Holy Spirit.[49]

In short, Murray was saying that the real ground of assurance is sanctification. A far cry, is it not, from the New Testament?

John Piper did not stray from the Puritan path, listing *twelve* aspects of the way believers get assurance. The third (citing 2 Cor. 13:5): 'Assurance cannot neglect the painful work of self-examination'. The sixth (citing Heb. 10:21-22): 'Repeated focusing on the sufficiency of the cross of Christ is crucial for assurance'. The tenth (citing Ps. 40:1-3): 'We must often wait patiently for the return of assurance'. The eleventh (1 Tim. 6:12): 'Assurance is a fight to the day we die'. And the last (citing Rom. 8:16 and 1 John

---

[48] Pink, quoting Baxter's *The Saint's Everlasting Rest*.
[49] John Murray pp270-274.

5:10-11) – the last, mark you: 'Assurance is finally a gift of the Spirit'.[50]

I will deal with 2 Corinthians 13:5 and show that Piper got it wrong.[51] As for Psalm 40:1-3, did Piper make a fair application of David's words? I think it far more likely that David was speaking of his conversion, or delivery from some trial – but I see no suggestion that he was struggling over assurance. As for 1 Timothy 6:12, I fail to see that it justifies Piper's heading.

And then we come to John Macarthur:

I think it's fair to say the pulpit is *rightly* the creator of anxious hearts. That's part of the duty of the preacher – to make the heart anxious. Why? So that, as 2 Corinthians 13:5 says, you examine yourself to see whether you're in the faith. [It] would be a breach of ministerial responsibility, it would be a forfeiture of the duty we have before God, to let people live comfortably and [have] an illusion about their true spiritual condition... The pulpit is to be a purveyor of a message that creates anxious hearts... Where there is that strong preaching, there will be a battle with assurance. And I'll tell you something, it's not bad to have that; it's good because how else are we drawn to the important issue of self-examination?[52]

Bear in mind that Macarthur was saying this to believers – not to the ungodly – and doing so in a sermon to give them assurance! Preachers, I agree, must preach so as to awaken and disturb *unbelievers* – but, as I say, Macarthur was here trying to help believers who are afraid and lacking assurance. Fantastic!

I would not be misunderstood. I am not saying that preachers should never disturb believers. Of course not! 2 Timothy 3:16, on its own, is more than sufficient to put a stop to that kind of talk. No! What is more, I define preaching as 'a confrontation' (Ezek. 16:2; 20:4; 22:2; 23:36),[53] and I deplore the fact that many preachers

---

[50] 'Helping People Have the Assurance of Salvation' (desiringgod.org). Another at the same website was entitled: 'The Agonizing Problem of the Assurance of Salvation'. What an uninviting title! Beeke's 'Quest' is bad enough!

[51] See Appendix 4.

[52] 'Why Christians Lack Assurance' (gty.org), emphasis mine. Macarthur said more, of course, but he did say this.

[53] But many versions have 'judge' instead of confront. Nevertheless, 'confront' is the right word. How often the prophets proclaimed *against*

steer as far away as possible from challenging believers, let alone upsetting or offending them. But, surely, when a man is deliberately setting out to remove a believer's fears over assurance, the last thing he should be doing is making believers harrow themselves, asserting that his job is to make them anxious.

When all this is played out in today's culture of inclusivism at all costs, we might well end up with preachers making saints anxious and, at the same time, lulling the unconverted to sleep! I know what MacArthur was doing, but in rightly trying to disturb 'the carnal Christian', I wonder how many *true and sincere believers* he made – and continues to make – unnecessarily anxious! James Sawyer commented:

---

people for their sins. The complaint of the people against Jeremiah was that he proclaimed against them (Jer. 1:18; 25:30; 26:11-12,20; 28:8). He was, of course, doing as God himself and as God commanded him (many verses). As for the verses from Ezekiel, Calvin commented: Judging 'embraces within itself all reproaches and threats. On the whole, since they acted deceitfully, and by no means proposed to submit themselves to God, hence he uses this bitterness: "What! are they worthy of your judging them? that is, of your contending with them?" For the prophet's duty is to argue with sinners, to threaten them, and to cite them to God's tribunal. God, therefore, pronounces them unworthy of such disputing, because they are not only deaf, but, hardened by abandoned obstinacy'. Gill: 'Will you not reprove and correct them, judge and condemn them, for their sins and wickedness?... Will you do your work and office as a prophet? Have you courage enough to do it? Will you rebuke and reprove?... Will you examine her [Israel's] case, judge truly, and condemn her, as you ought to do? Have you inclination to take this affair in hand? Then be directed to it, as follows:.. You shall show her all her abominations; lay them before her; convict her of them; show her the evil of them, and the punishment they deserve; every kind of sin she was guilty of. For, as for particular acts, it was impossible to reckon them; those sins that were the most flagrant, and most frequently committed, and which were abominable to the Lord, and rendered her so in his sight, are intended. This you ought to do... Do as follows... declare unto them their abominations, their abominable sins, their murders, adulteries, and idolatries. Set them in a true light before them, in all their aggravated circumstances, that, if it can be, they may be brought to a true sight and sense of them, to repent of them, be ashamed of them, loathe them, confess them, and forsake them'. See my 'Confronting The Cultures' and my 'The True Minister:1' (David H J Gay Ministry sermonaudio.com).

[Macarthur] contends: 'When a man obeys God he gives *the only possible evidence* that in his heart he believes God'. Elsewhere, MacArthur notes that since salvation is a work of God, it is God who produces the fruit of salvation in us, noting that any professed salvation which lacks any of the elements of salvation is to be found wanting from a biblical perspective. *The practical effect of such teaching is to suspend assurance of salvation* (not salvation itself) upon performance – works. The net effect is to destroy the confidence that the believer is commanded in Scripture to have before God. The dynamic of assurance espoused by Dr. MacArthur has its roots deep in the tradition of the Puritans and the Scottish Calvinists. The Scots referred to this process as: 'The Practical Syllogism'. The Puritans called it: 'The Reflex Action'. By whatever name, the process is the same. The believer is denied direct access to the Saviour for assurance. Instead he must look inside and complete the syllogism: 'The Scripture tells me that he who believes shall be saved. If upon examining myself I find fruits of righteousness in my life, I may then complete the syllogism But I believe, therefore I shall be saved'. However, such a doctrine lays the ground of assurance solely within ourselves causing the believer to rely more on his own works for assurance, than on the work of Christ on our behalf. The ultimate result of such teaching is uncertainty.[54]

I leave the extracts there. So much for legal assurance. Give me the New Testament variety, every time!

---

[54] Sawyer.

Conclusion

According to the New Testament, everyone who believes God's promise in the gospel, and trusts Christ, has the Spirit. He must have the Spirit (John 14:17; Rom. 8:9; 1 Cor. 12:13). He could only have believed by the power of the Spirit (John 6:44; Eph. 2:8). Furthermore, the Spirit having enabled the sinner to believe, then indwells him (John 14:17; Rom. 8:9; 1 Cor. 3:16; 1 John 4:13), taking away his fear, giving him the spirit of sonship, enabling him to call God his Father, sealing him, anointing him, and witnessing with his spirit that he is indeed a child of God, having adopted him into his family. In this way, the believer is assured, and given inexpressible joy and glory, with an increasing sense of it (Rom. 8:9-17; 2 Cor. 1:21-22; 2 Cor. 3:18; Gal. 3:26 – 4:7; 5:1,13; Eph. 1:13-14; 4:30; 1 Pet. 1:8; 1 John 2:20-27; 3:24; 4:13; 5:6,9-11, for instance). All this was true of New Testament believers.

For the majority of believers today, however, talk like this is virtually a foreign language; worse, it is a foreign experience, at least consciously speaking. Indeed, even to talk like this is almost certain to bring the dismissing retort: 'Charismatic!' If so, let me remind you, reader, of the apostle's warnings: 'Do not grieve the Holy Spirit of God, with whom you were sealed for the day of redemption' (Eph. 4:30).[1] 'Do not put out the Spirit's fire' (1 Thess. 5:19).[2] And fire, warmth, the burning heart, is precisely what the

---

[1] Gill: Believers grieve the Holy Spirit 'especially when they entertain any undervaluing [thoughts] of Jesus Christ, whose glorifier he is'.

[2] Matthew Henry: 'We quench the Spirit if we do not stir up our spirits, and all that is within us, to comply with the motions of the good Spirit'. Calvin: 'The meaning... is: "Be enlightened by the Spirit of God. See that you do not lose that light through your ingratitude". This is an exceedingly useful admonition... We must, therefore, be on our guard against indolence, by which the light of God is choked in us... It is our part to ask from the Lord, that he would furnish oil to the lamps which he has lighted up, that he may keep the wick pure, and may even increase it'. Gill thought the apostle may have been referring to 'the graces of the Spirit, which may be compared to light, and fire, and heat, to which the allusion is in the text: such as faith, which is a light in the soul, a seeing of the Son, and an

downcast disciples experienced on the road to Emmaus when Christ revealed himself to them through the Scriptures (Luke 24:32). And it is this warmth which believers should have today. Sadly, however, most believers seem to have lost it.

For some, assurance has become largely a matter of the mind, little to do with the heart. Too often, having been presented with facts, mere facts, facts which we believe – that is, assent to them, or, in the words of N.T.Wright, 'learn our lines and join in the drama' – we end up with so-called 'assurance'; *and that, for many, is as far as it goes.* And this, if assent is all it is, is not saving. Many preachers, wishing to avoid this sorry state in their hearers, instruct converts to pore over their works, promising them the possibility (but not the probability or likelihood) of assurance after years of struggle. Rarely, these days, does the teacher speak of the inner witness, the burning heart. Too often, as I say, any mention of an emotional heart-warming, or talk of the Spirit's inner witness, sealing or anointing, is frowned upon as charismaticism – and dismissed.

How is it that New Testament believers enjoyed this assurance, yet many of us today do not? As I said right at the start, the weakening of our hold on the new covenant – to put it no stronger – is a major contributing factor in this. More! It's not our hold on the new covenant which is wanted; it's the new covenant's grip on us! Many today, however, instead of sitting under those who preach the gospel, are listening to men who preach law – overtly, the Mosaic law; incipiently, rules and regulations – and in this way are being taught into doubt, introspection, bondage and sadness. By law preachers I mean those who mistakenly preach the law to sinners to so-say prepare them for Christ, and bring them to him, who then go

---

evidence of things not seen; and love, which gives a vehement flame, which many waters cannot quench; and zeal, which is the boiling up of love, the fervency of it; and spiritual knowledge, which is also light, and of an increasing nature, and are all graces of the Spirit. And though these cannot be totally extinguished, and utterly put out and lost, yet they may be greatly damped. The light of faith may become dim, and the flame of love be abated, and that wax cold. The heat of zeal may pass into lukewarmness, and an indifference of spirit. And the light of knowledge seem to decline instead of increasing'.

on to preach the law to saints to make them sanctified, and hence to gain some sort of assurance. And all the while they should be preaching Christ – preaching Christ to sinners and saints, preaching Christ for every grace.

It is not just I saying it. I get it from Paul. He said that 'Christ is all' (Col. 3:11). Listen to him, speaking when he was languishing in prison, and could not preach – in the usual sense of the word. He knew that others, outside the prison, were taking advantage of his confinement. Some were rubbing salt into his wounds. Others, emboldened by his example, were preaching more fearlessly than before. And Paul rejoiced! Why? Whether men were preaching to mock and hurt him, or were preaching to follow his example, the apostle rejoiced, because, as he said, 'the word of God' is preached, 'the gospel' is preached; above all, as he said: 'Christ is preached' (Phil. 1:12-18). Is this not clear enough? Christ is preached! This is what made the apostle tick, this is what made him rejoice. We must, therefore, preach Christ!

If this is not sufficiently convincing, consider Paul's declaration to the Corinthians:

We preach Christ crucified... Christ the power of God and the wisdom of God... Christ Jesus, who has become for us wisdom from God – that is, our righteousness, holiness and redemption... I resolved to know nothing while I was with you except Jesus Christ and him crucified (1 Cor. 1:23-24,30; 2:2).

As the apostle went on to tell them: 'Yet when I preach the gospel, I cannot boast, for I am compelled to preach. Woe to me if I do not preach the gospel!' (1 Cor. 9:16). Do not miss the point: this was Paul's consistent practice, whether addressing sinners or saints. He always preached Christ; he never preached anyone or anything else! He did not preach a creed. He did not preach a confession or a catechism. He preached the word of God, the Scriptures. And that means he preached Christ, for Christ is in all the Scriptures (Luke 24:27,32). See 1 Corinthians 15:1-11. Paul preached Christ as Lord (2 Cor. 4:5). Christ, not law! He did not preach the law to non-Gentile unbelievers,[3] and he never preached the law to believers.

---

[3] The apostles used the law when addressing unconverted Jews, since the Jews were familiar with it. But they were prepared to use anything to

He would mention the law to them (Rom. 13:8-10; Gal. 5:14; Eph. 6:1-4), and use it as an illustration or paradigm (model or pattern), yes, but he always preached Christ. Take those very verses. Read the passages which precede and follow them. What do you find? The apostle never allowed his use of the law to compromise his focus, his theme: Christ! As he told the Ephesian elders:

You know that I have not hesitated to preach anything that would be helpful to you but have taught you publicly and from house to house. I have declared to both Jews and Greeks that they must turn to God in repentance and have faith in our Lord Jesus... I consider my life worth nothing to me, if only I may finish the race and complete the task the Lord Jesus has given me – the task of testifying to the gospel of God's grace... I declare to you today that I am innocent of the blood of all men. For I have not hesitated to proclaim to you the whole will of God... I commit you to God and to the word of his grace, which can build you up and give you an inheritance among all those who are sanctified (Acts 20:20-32).

There is a direct connection between this kind of preaching and the way sinners were converted and enjoyed assurance in New Testament days. And I say there is a connection, today, between legal preaching and our lack of assurance.[4] The last day will declare it.

In short, assurance comes, not by harrowing introspection, raking over one's sanctification, but by the witness of the Spirit. This is the apostolic testimony.

But what about these passages (in 1 and 2 Corinthians, 2 Peter and 1 John) which call the believer to self-examination, and the like, in order to assure himself? Don't they fly in the face of what I

---

illustrate what they were saying. The fact that they never used the law when addressing Gentile unbelievers showed their wisdom – why use something of which their hearers knew nothing? More, it makes my point. Gentiles were converted to Christ without the use of the law. It cannot be necessary therefore, to preach the law to the unconverted. The law does not prepare sinners for Christ. In any case, sinners do not need to be prepared or made fit for Christ!

[4] It could even be that 'conversion' is a casualty of today's preaching. Preaching law, especially in its incipient form, can so easily produce conformity and not conversion – fatal!

have asserted? They do not! See Appendices 3 – 6, where I make good my case.

What about: 'Work out your salvation with fear and trembling' (Phil. 2:12)? Surely, seeing believers have to 'fear' and 'tremble', they can hardly be said to be assured, can they? This, of course, is to completely misread the apostle's meaning in that verse. Look at its context for a start. Paul is saying that believers are never to become smug, self-confident and careless. He's not remotely calling believers to doubt their assurance in Christ!

Calvin, commenting on the verse, spoke of the Papists who:

...pervert this passage so as to shake the assurance of faith, for the man that trembles is in uncertainty. They, accordingly, understand Paul's words as if they meant that we ought, during our whole life, to waver as to assurance of salvation. If, however, we would not have Paul contradict himself, he does not by any means exhort us to hesitation, inasmuch as he everywhere recommends confidence and full assurance. The solution, however, is easy, if anyone is desirous of attaining the true meaning [of the passage] without any spirit of contention. There are two kinds of fear; the one produces anxiety along with humility; the other hesitation. The former is opposed to fleshly confidence and carelessness, equally as to arrogance; the latter, to assurance of faith. Further, we must take notice, that, as believers repose with assurance upon the grace of God, so, when they direct their views to their own frailty, they do not by any means resign themselves carelessly to sleep, but are by fear of dangers stirred up to prayer. Yet, so far is this fear from disturbing tranquillity of conscience, and shaking confidence, that it rather confirms it. For distrust of ourselves leads us to lean more confidently upon the mercy of God. And this is what Paul's words import, for he requires nothing from the Philippians, but that they submit themselves to God with true self-renunciation.

Calvin's words ought to be weighed – not least by those who profess to hold him in high regard: 'Believers [must] repose with assurance upon the grace of God', and not 'direct their views to their own frailty'; that is, their sanctification.

In bringing my book to a conclusion, I think I can do no better than spell out – once again! – what is at stake, and what is NOT at stake, in all that I have said.

Let me start with the negative. Sanctification is not at issue. Sanctification, godliness of life is essential. If a professing believer is not sanctified, he is showing that he is not justified. While sanctification does not contribute to our justification, it is an essential and inevitable concomitant and outcome of justification. In all their letters, the apostles wrote to believers, and urged them to greater godliness – in line with the categorical assertion that sanctification is essential and inevitable for the true child of God (2 Cor. 5:17). Thus, if a man has no interest in sanctification, he is demonstrating that he is not saved. There can be no happiness without holiness, since 'without holiness no one will see the Lord' (Heb. 12:14). Sanctification is essential.

Sanctification is also necessary for other believers to recognise the converted: there is no promise that the Spirit will bear witness with your spirit that I am converted. I can only show you that by my life:

By their fruit you will recognise them. Do people pick grapes from thorn bushes, or figs from thistles? Likewise every good tree bears good fruit, but a bad tree bears bad fruit. A good tree cannot bear bad fruit, and a bad tree cannot bear good fruit... Thus, by their fruit you will recognise them (Matt. 7:16-20).

Sanctification also serves as a secondary confirmation for believers who have, for some reason or another, lost their assurance.[5]

No believer is perfect in this life. Sinless perfection, this side of glory, is found only in Christ.

Every believer will suffer persecution, meet trouble, be faced with temptations, come into affliction, and have questions, difficulties and doubts.

None of that is at issue.

And now for the positive. Assurance is primarily by the witness of the Spirit, not by sanctification. It is a fact – a fact, I say – that every believer in the New Testament, at conversion, was joined to Christ, included in Christ, had his spirit of fear removed, received the Spirit of adoption, and had the witness of the Spirit. Every believer had all this, and had it *before* any sanctification could possibly have taken place. And this means that New Testament

---

[5] For Calvin on this, see Appendix 2.

believers were assured, not by their sanctification, but by the witness of the Spirit.

Yes, through bad or false teaching – maybe in other ways too – some New Testament believers lost their assurance, but the apostles did not write to tell them that this was what they must expect! They didn't tell them that only a favoured few ever get assurance, and most of them get it only on their death-bed! No! Far from encouraging them to go on struggling with their doubt, they wrote to restore those doubting believers to their former joy, and restore them at once, there and then.[6] And they did it, above all, by taking them back to Christ and free grace. This is the very thing Paul did when addressing the Galatians: he took them back to where they began and where they had left the right road (Gal. 3:1-5). One thing is certain: no apostle ever sought to 'help' doubting believers by preaching introspection and law.

Every preacher ought to take heed to what Calvin said when commenting on 1 John 5:13-14 – and do it! I stress the relevant passage:

But we ought to observe the way in which faith is confirmed, even by having the office and power of Christ explained to us. For the apostle says that he wrote these things, that is, that eternal life is to be sought nowhere else but in Christ, in order that they who were believers already might believe, that is, make progress in believing. *It is therefore the duty of a godly teacher, in order to confirm disciples in the faith, to extol as much as possible the grace of Christ, so that being satisfied with that, we may seek nothing else.*

Believers who are instructed to look to their sanctification for assurance, are, therefore, being seriously misdirected. They are traversing an unscriptural track. Misguidedly struggling to gain assurance by probing their works, they are on a course which is bound to leave them in constant suspense. Who can say his sanctification is perfect? Who has enough sanctification? Who can say his sanctification is good enough for assurance? Sadness and bondage must be the result for any sensitive, thinking believer.

Let me illustrate by my own experience. When I was a young believer, I knew I didn't blaspheme, I wasn't committing adultery, I

---

[6] See Appendix 3.

wasn't getting drunk, I never drank. 'I'm a good, spiritual man!', I might have thought. But it wasn't long before I began to see things in a very different light. And now, many years later, I certainly know that's not all there is to it – no, not by a long chalk! There are sins, maybe greater sins, which are more secret, more inward: pride, arrogance, jealousy, bitterness, grudge-bearing, impatience, covetousness, prejudice, resentment, and the like. Am I guilty of them? And what about motive? I preach. Why do I preach? Do I preach faithfully? Do I preach to myself first? Do I always take my own medicine? Where's my heart? How's my heart? What about hypocrisy? And so on and on. Do you see what I mean? In the beginning, it's drunkenness and blasphemy and external sins. Now, it's... I'll never get to the end of it! In myself, I'm a sinner through and through, and if I look within, what do I see? Do I see enough spirituality? Do I have sufficient evidence to show me that I am a believer, that I am a *true* believer, a *sincere* believer, a *strong* believer, a *consistent* believer, a believer with sanctification good enough to make me certain that I'm a true believer? Speaking for myself, I simply cannot discover any hope for assurance by my sanctification. So much for me. Reader, what about you?

But if, following the path marked out by the apostles, the believer is taught and encouraged to look to Christ, Christ bearing witness in his heart through his Holy Spirit, the Spirit bearing witness to Christ, and glorifying him to the believer, bearing witness to all the glories the believer has in his free justification in Christ, well, then assurance is the result!

Let me return to Richard Baxter. You will recall that I used his testimony to observe how legal preaching brings bondage. Now listen to him pointing to the remedy:

For those doubts of my own salvation, which exercised me many years, the chiefest causes of them were these... because I could not distinctly trace the workings of the Spirit upon my heart in that method which Mr Bolton, Mr Hooker, Mr Rogers, and other divines describe... I was once [inclined] to meditate on my own heart... I was continually poring either on my sins or wants, or examining my sincerity... *but now, though I am greatly convinced of the need of heart-acquaintance... yet I see more need of a higher work, and that I should look often upon Christ, and God, and heaven, [rather] than upon my own heart.*[7]

And what about my epigraph? 'And the disciples were filled with joy and with the Holy Spirit' (Acts 13:52). I have no doubt about the reason! Doesn't the New Testament teach that God decreed the salvation of his elect in eternity past, that he sent his Son into the world to live and die for them in order to save them? Doesn't it teach that the elect, having been brought by the Spirit to repentance and faith, are perfectly, fully and absolutely justified – free of sin and clothed with the righteousness of Christ, without fault or stain, and utterly beyond condemnation? And doesn't it teach that the believer, contemplating Christ, contemplating his own perfection in Christ, is moved to seek to live to the glory of the triune God who planned, accomplished and applies salvation to him? Doesn't it teach that when the believer gets to glory, God will reward him for his good works done out of his gratitude to God for his love, grace and mercy?[8] Doesn't the New Testament teach that the believer has died to sin, law and death, and is alive to God, fruitful to God, liberated and empowered, and has ever increasing glory and unspeakable joy, and has it now? And, in the midst of all this, immediately at the point of faith and union with Christ, doesn't the Spirit bear witness with the believer, seal him and anoint him? Doesn't all this bring assurance? And doesn't all this feed on itself? A *gracious* circle, indeed!

As William Hammond put it:

We are not to live upon the sanctification that is wrought in us, but the sanctification that is in Christ. Otherwise, we shall live upon the streams instead of the fountain... They are truly happy who live by the faith of the Son of God. Blessed are they who see Christ their all in all, and who see nothing at all, indeed, and desire to see nothing at all but Christ alone. While the eye of the soul is steadily fixed on Christ, that soul is perfectly happy, so happy that it cannot be happier, unless in the full fruition of Christ in glory. But the moment we take our eye off from Christ, and look after something else beside the Lord Christ, that moment, I say, our souls are unsettled, confused and distressed. We then become quite uneasy, and utterly miserable; nor can we find any

---

[7] Baxter pp10,113, emphasis mine.

[8] Not that the works merit salvation, of course, but they do bring reward.

comfort or satisfaction till we return to our rest; that is, to Christ... Never turn your eye from Christ any more, but keep looking to him continually. Behold him as the author and finisher of your faith; look upon him as the alpha and omega, the first and the last, the beginning and end of your salvation (Heb. 12:1; Rev. 1:8,11). And look at nothing else, either within you or without you, but Christ; for in him you are complete (Col. 2:10); in him you are perfect (Col. 1:28); in him you are washed, in him you are sanctified, in him you are justified (1 Cor. 6:11). He is made unto us of God, wisdom, righteousness, sanctification and redemption (1 Cor. 1:30). In him we are perfect and entire, wanting nothing (Jas. 1:4). And this is properly Christian perfection, because indeed this perfection is not inherent in us, but it subsists in Christ, and is ours only by virtue of our union with Christ. Every Christian, truly so called, is one with Christ (1 Cor. 6:17), and therefore purifies himself even as he is pure (1 John 3:3). He is righteous even as he [Christ] is righteous (1 John 3:7). He is merciful as God is merciful (Luke 6:36). He is holy as God is holy (1 Pet. 1:15-16). He is perfect as his Father which is in heaven is perfect (Matt. 5:48).[9]

Reader, are you looking to the law – or to Christ? Are you looking to your works for assurance – or to Jesus? Are you a preacher? Do you preach Christ? Preach him, not law! Preach Christ!

As William Gadsby expressed it:

Immortal honours rest on Jesus' head;
My God, my portion, and my living bread;
In him I live, upon him cast my care;
He saves from death, destruction, and despair.

He is my refuge in each deep distress;
The Lord my strength and glorious righteousness;
Through floods and flames he leads me safely on,
And daily makes his sovereign goodness known.

My every need he richly will supply;
Nor will his mercy ever let me die;
In him there dwells a treasure all divine,
And matchless grace has made that treasure mine.

---

[9] Hammond xxi-xxiv.

Conclusion

O that my soul could love and praise him more,
His beauties trace, his majesty adore;
Live near his heart, upon his bosom lean;
Obey his voice, and all his will esteem.

And Horatius Bonar:

I bless the Christ of God,
I rest on love divine,
And with unfaltering lip and heart,
I call this Saviour mine.

His cross dispels each doubt
I bury in his tomb
Each thought of unbelief and fear,
Each lingering shade of gloom.

I praise the God of peace,
I trust his truth and might;
He calls me his, I call him mine,
My God, my joy, my light.

In him is only good,
In me is only ill;
My ill but draws his goodness forth,
And me he loveth still.

'Tis he who saveth me,
And freely pardon gives;
I love because he loveth me;
I live because he lives.

My life with him is hid,
My death has passed away,
My clouds have melted into light,
My midnight into day.

To those who still doubt, and still wonder how all this could cure them of their lack of assurance, let me try once more. The witness of the Spirit with your spirit – how and what does he witness to? Christ! Now then tell me: What do you think of Jesus? What has the Spirit enabled you to think and say about Jesus? Is he precious to you? Let me return to a verse to which I have already referred. Peter is adamant: 'To you who believe, [the Lord Jesus Christ] is precious' (1 Pet. 2:7). Let me put it the other way about: 'Those who believe call Jesus precious'. Jesus is precious. Can you say that? You can? Can you say: 'Jesus is precious to me'? You can? Well... how can you say that – except by the Spirit? 'I tell you that no one who is speaking by the Spirit of God says: "Jesus be cursed", and no one can say: "Jesus is Lord", except by the Holy Spirit' (1 Cor. 12:3). We are not teaching parrots! Nor am I taking Wright's advice and teaching you to 'learn your lines'! Now then, will you give up following the prescription of the law men, and believe the apostles instead? Will you now agree that God's Spirit has borne witness with your spirit, glorifying Christ to you, making him precious to you? In your heart, do you not know that Jesus is precious? Can you not now *say* that Christ is yours and you are his? *Will* you not say it? 'Mine, mine, mine,/ I know thou art mine'. You may feel you have to say: 'I do believe; help me overcome my unbelief!' (Mark 9:24), but you can, at least, now say that you believe. Will you?[10]

I would address all hyper-Calvinists in the same vein. It is not presumption to take this road. If you persist in following your teachers and trotting out the pejorative word, remember to whom you are saying it! Not me! Peter!

Christ is precious to you? Then listen to Newton, writing on the question posed by Christ : 'What do you think about the Christ?' (Matt. 22:42): 'What think ye of Christ is the test/ To try both your state and your scheme'. If, in Newton's words, you 'think rightly' of Jesus, if Jesus is precious to you, only the Spirit of God could have taught you thus (John 6:44-47). And only the Spirit could have taught you to agree with Peter: you could go to no one else but Christ, for, as you know, he alone has the words of eternal life (John 6:67-69).

---

[10] It has been put to me that in saying this I am returning to assurance by evidences. Not so. John, writing to those who have lost their assurance, appeals to the evidences of regeneration – evidence that a third party has to use – to take them back to joy. Yes, he first argues his case doctrinally, primarily making emphatic testimony to the anointing with the Spirit – but he also is prepared to fall back on these secondary supports. By extension (living with that which was unknown to John – Christendom – to which I have already referred), I am doing something similar (see 1 John 1:7-10; 2:23; 4:2-3,15-16; 5:1-5,10-13,20-21). See also Appendix 3.

Conclusion

Jesus is precious to you? Then listen to Spurgeon:

You cannot see Christ by mere reason, for the natural man is blind to the things of the Spirit... You will never get to see the real Christ who is precious to believers except by a personal act of faith in him. The Holy Spirit has removed the scales from the eyes of the man who believes... Our sense of Christ's preciousness... is a proof of our possessing the faith of God's elect – and this ought to be a great comfort to any of you who are in the habit of looking within. If you enquire within yourselves: 'Is my faith worked in my soul by the Holy Spirit?' you may have a sure test. Does it magnify Christ? If it makes Christ inexpressibly dear to you it is the faith of God's elect.

Spurgeon moved on to help his hearers nurture their sense of assurance:

May God grant you to have more of it! Christ becomes growingly precious to us as our faith grows. If you have faith in Christ but do not exercise it every day he will not be very precious to you. But if your faith keeps her eyes fixed on him, she will more and more clearly perceive his beauties. If your soul is driven to Jesus again and again – if your faith anchors in him continually – then he will be, indeed, more and more precious to you. Everything depends upon faith. If you doubt Christ, he has gone down fifty per cent in your esteem. Every doubt is a Christ crucifier. Every time you give way to scepticism and critical questioning you lose a sip of sweetness... The Christian that disputes loses spiritual food. In proportion as you believe with a faith which is childlike, clear, simple, strong, unbroken – in that proportion will Christ be dearer and dearer to you! I recommend you to keep the door of your mind on the chain in these days – for those tramps and vagrants called doubts are prowling about in every quarter – and they may knock at your door with vile intent. The first thing they say, when they are at a good man's door, is: 'I am an honest doubt'. That which so loudly calls itself honest has good need to fabricate for itself a character. The most honest doubt is a great thief – the most of doubts are as dishonest as common housebreakers. Keep doubt out of the soul or you will make small progress in the discovery of the preciousness of Christ. Never entertain a thought that is derogatory to Christ's person, or to his atoning sacrifice. Reckon that opinion to be your enemy which is the enemy of the cross of Christ. Do not suffer your faith to diminish even in the least degree. Believe in Christ heartily and unsuspectingly! If you have a doubt as to whether you are a saint – you can have no question that you are a sinner – come to Christ as a sinner and put your trust in him as your Saviour! It is wonderful how a renewed confidence in Christ's saving grace will bring back all your joy and delight in him, and sometimes do it at once... God grant you, dear brothers and sisters, by faith, to know the preciousness of Christ – for only to you that believe is he precious! To you that doubt, to you that mistrust, to you that suspect, to you that live in the land of hesitation he is without form or comeliness – but to you that believe without doubt he is precious beyond all price.[11]

Martin Luther was another who did what he could to help believers avoid getting into doubt, or bring them out if they had been plunged into it. This was his sound – biblical – advice:

Train your conscience to believe that God approves of you. Fight it out with doubt. Gain assurance through the word of God. Say: 'I am all right with God. I have the Holy Ghost. Christ, in whom I do believe, makes me worthy...'...

I pause. Luther was right. This is what the Bible teaches. As believers, we must learn to speak to ourselves, in order to remind ourselves of the truth; we have to think biblically about ourselves. As Paul, writing to the Romans on another issue at that time, told them: 'Count yourselves dead to sin but alive to God in Christ Jesus' (Rom. 6:11). 'Count yourselves'? 'Consider yourselves' (NASB); 'Reckon yourselves' (AV, NKJV). The verb is *logizomai*,[12] a rich word derived from *logos*, 'reason in terms of speaking or thinking', meaning 'to reckon inwardly, count up or weigh the reasons, to deliberate, by reckoning up all the reasons, to gather or infer, to meditate on with a view to obtaining something, to suppose, deem, judge, to think', and so on.[13] Let me list some examples of the various ways in which it is used:

They *discussed* it among themselves and said... (Mark 11:31).
I *consider* that our present sufferings are not worth comparing with the glory that will be revealed in us (Rom. 8:18).
So then, men ought to *regard* us as servants of Christ (1 Cor. 4:1).
Not that we are competent in ourselves to *claim* anything for ourselves, but our competence comes from God (2 Cor. 3:5).

---

[11] Sermon number 2137.
[12] A favourite word of Paul. He used it 27 times (not counting quotations) whereas the rest of the New Testament uses it only four times.
[13] Thayer.

I beg you that when I come I may not have to be as bold as I *expect* to be toward some people who *think* that we live by the standards of this world (2 Cor. 10:2).

Finally, brothers, whatever is true, whatever is noble, whatever is right, whatever is pure, whatever is lovely, whatever is admirable – if anything is excellent or praiseworthy – *think* about such things (Phil.4:8).

Paul counselled believers to think, to reason, to reckon in this way; in other words, to apply the truth to themselves, to their consciences. Luther was right, therefore. This is how we, as believers, should treat all gospel truth: we should think in this way, reason in this way, consider ourselves in the light of it, apply it to ourselves, talk to ourselves about it, talk to others about it: 'Train your conscience to believe that God approves of you. Fight it out with doubt. Gain assurance through the word of God. Say: 'I am all right with God. I have the Holy Ghost. Christ, in whom I do believe, makes me worthy'.

If I may illustrate. As I understand it, artificial hearing aids pick up all sounds and give them equal weight. In our natural hearing, however, the brain distinguishes the sound it wishes to hear. So it is here. In all the clamour of law, sanctification, calls for introspection, the harrowing quest for assurance and the agonising search for it, with which we are bombarded, we must learn to distinguish the still small voice of the Spirit. And the more we discern his voice, the more we train ourselves to listen to him, the more we reason in this way, the more we read Scripture in this way, the more we hear preaching on this theme, the more we talk to ourselves in this way, then the more distinctly we shall hear the Spirit bearing witness with our spirit that we are indeed the children of God.

To let Luther go on:

Let the law, sin, and the devil cry out against us until their outcry fills heaven and earth. The Spirit of God outcries them all. Our feeble groans: 'Abba, Father', will be heard of God sooner than the combined racket of hell, sin, and the law... Let us not fail to thank God for delivering us from the doctrine of doubt. The gospel commands us to look away from our own good works to the promises of God in Christ, the Mediator... Let us never doubt the mercy of God in Christ Jesus, but make up our minds that God is pleased with us, that he looks after us, and that we have the Holy Spirit who prays for us... The apostle always has Christ on the tip of his tongue... He talks of Christ continually. As often as he speaks of righteousness, grace, the promise, the adoption, and the inheritance of heaven, he adds the words 'in Christ', or 'through Christ', to show that these blessings are not to be had by the law, or the deeds of the law, much less by our own exertions, or by the observance of human traditions, but only by and through and in Christ.[14]

Charles Wesley, speaking of the Holy Spirit:

True witness of my sonship, now
Engraving pardon on my heart,
Seal of my sin in Christ forgiven,
Earnest of love, and pledge of heaven.
Come, then, my God, mark out thine heir;
Of heaven a larger earnest give;
With clearer light thy witness bear,
More sensibly within me live;
Let all my powers thine entrance feel
And deeper stamp thyself the seal.

Let the apostle have the last word. Reader, while not remotely claiming to be standing in his boots, I have written as I have because as Paul declares:

I want you to know what a great conflict I have for you [at Colossae] and those in Laodicea, and for as many as have not seen my face in the flesh, that their hearts may be encouraged, being knit together in love, and attaining to all riches of the full assurance of understanding, to the knowledge of the mystery of God, both of the Father and of Christ, in whom are hidden all the treasures of wisdom and knowledge. Now this I say lest anyone should deceive you with persuasive words. For though I am absent in the flesh, yet I am with you in spirit, rejoicing to see your good order and the steadfastness of your faith in Christ. As you have therefore received Christ Jesus the Lord, so walk in him, rooted and built up in him and established in the faith, as you have been taught, abounding in it with thanksgiving. Beware lest anyone cheat you through philosophy and empty deceit, according to the

---

[14] Luther commenting on Gal. 4:6-7. Luther was ambiguous as to whether assurance is essential, but, according to R.L.Dabney, he was more scriptural than Calvin (see Beeke: 'Martin Luther on Assurance'). Alas, as so often with Luther, he wrongly linked this to baptism.

Conclusion

tradition of men, according to the basic principles of the world, and not according to Christ. For in him dwells all the fullness of the Godhead bodily; and you are complete in him, who is the head of all principality and power... Christ is all, and is in all (Col. 2:1-10; 3:11, NKJV).

Appendices

Appendix 1
'The Essence of Faith'

This phrase, 'the essence of faith', continues to play an important role in the way men think about assurance. Some say that assurance is the essence of faith. Others deny it. Who is right? Is assurance the essence of faith?

I am sure it is not. But...

First of all, what is 'essence'? We could use such words as 'core, spirit, heart, real meaning, quintessence, soul, fundamental nature'; the essence is the basic nature of a thing, the quality or qualities that make it what it is. Now assurance, whatever it is, is not the real meaning of faith, it does not define faith. Assurance lies very close to the heart of faith, and it certainly accompanies faith, but it is not its essence. The essence of faith is 'trust'. Assurance, brought about by the witness of the Spirit, by the seal of the Spirit, by the anointing with the Spirit, is a concomitant of faith, it accompanies faith, it runs alongside faith, it is a consequence of faith – just as inclusion in Christ, justification, liberation from death, sin and the law, the removal of fear, the making of sinners into sons, adopting them into the family of God, the turning of rebels into heirs of God, and so on. All these are the concomitants and consequences of faith. And so is assurance. It is as the sinner trusts Christ that he receives all these benefits and graces of the Spirit, including assurance. But none of them are the essence of faith.

I'm certainly not saying that these graces and experiences are optional extras. Nor am I saying that some believers have some of them, but very few have them all. Certainly not! All these gifts and graces, all of them, always accompany saving faith. But they are not faith's essence. As I say, the core, the heart, the fundamental nature of saving faith is trust, trust in Christ. I am not playing with words. Making assurance the essence of faith goes beyond Scripture, leading to the inevitable conclusion that unless a man is assured he cannot be a true believer. This is quite wrong. For we know that some New Testament believers had lost their sense of assurance. Even so, they were believers – as John, in his first letter, wrote to assure them. While I recognise that their experience is not precisely the same as many of today's believers (who seem never to be assured), nevertheless John's teaching still can and must be applied to us today, as I showed in the body of my book.[1]

But a sense of assurance is not the only note which is often missing in the believer's consciousness today. Take some of the other accompaniments of faith: inclusion in Christ, liberation from the law, the turning of the enemies of God into his sons, the making of rebels into joint-heirs with Christ, and so on. Every believer is in Christ, every believer is freed from the law, every believer is a child of God, and so on, but, alas, not every believer has an active and vibrant sense of these things. Nevertheless, though such believers are impoverished, they are still believers. So it is with assurance.

In short, while the witness of the Spirit is not the essence of faith, it always accompanies saving faith – as much as union with Christ, justification and all the rest. The witness of the Spirit is given to every believer at conversion. Even so, assurance is not 'the essence of faith'.

---

[1] See the 'Conclusion'.

Appendix 2

New-Covenant Assurance: Supporting Testimonies

I do not quote the following to establish my position on assurance, but simply to show that others have said similar things to me. I recognise that some of the following writers may have said different things on other occasions, but at least, as I have quoted them here, they are, in the main, supportive of what I set out in the body of this book. I know that at least some of these writers held to the Reformed view of the law, but all I can say is that they were inconsistent: while mistaken on the law, they were right on assurance by the Spirit, at least in most of what I quote from them here.

James I. Packer spoke of John 16:14 as the key text, setting out the Spirit's 'work of making Jesus Christ, our crucified, risen reigning Saviour, real and glorious to us moment by moment'. He went on:

The Spirit's way of witnessing to the truth that as believers we are sons and heirs of God (Rom. 5:15-17) is first to make us realise that as Christ on earth loved us and died for us, so in glory now he loves us and lives for us as the Mediator whose endless life guarantees us endless glory with him. The Spirit makes us see the love of Christ towards us, as measured by the cross, and to see along with Christ's love the love of the Father who gave his Son up for us (Rom. 8:32)... Then, together with that, the Spirit makes us also see that through Christ, in Christ, and with Christ, we are now God's children; and hereby he leads us, spontaneously and instinctively... to think of God as Father, and so to address him (Rom. 8:15; Gal. 4:6)... To know that God is your Father and that he loves you, his adopted child, no less than he loves his only begotten Son and to know that enjoyment of God's love and glory for all eternity are [*sic*] pledged to you brings inward delight that is sometimes overwhelming; and this also is the Spirit's doing. For the 'joy in the Holy Spirit', in terms of which Paul defines the kingdom of God in Romans 14:17, is the 'rejoicing in God' spoken of in Romans 5:2,11, and it is the Spirit's witness to God's love for us that calls forth this joy...

Paul speaks of the Spirit's witness in the present tense (... 'testifies'...), implying that it is a continuous operation that imparts permanent confidence in God. Though not always felt as vividly as it is sometimes, and though overshadowed from time to time by feelings of doubt and despair, this confidence remains constant and, in the final analysis, insuperable. The Spirit himself sees to that!

...The Holy Spirit given to us is the 'earnest' of our inheritance in this precise sense: that by enabling us to see the glory of Christ glorified, and to live in fellowship with him as our Mediator, and with his Father as our Father, the Spirit introduces us to the inmost essence of life in heaven... to see God and to be forever with Christ in an experiential deepening of heaven (see Matt. 5:8; 2 Cor. 5:6-8; 1 Thess. 4:7; Rev. 22:3-5). And by means of the ministry to us of the indwelling Spirit heaven begins for us here and now, as through Christ and in Christ we are made sharers with Christ of his resurrection life... (Col. 3:3; see Col. 2:11-14; Rom. 6:3-11; Eph. 2:1-7).[1]

Ernest Kevan:

A conviction is born within us that we are the sons of God: this is our own conviction, but it is as well the conviction of the Holy Spirit who is within us. It is this 'joint-witness' of the Holy Spirit and our own spirit. It thus conforms to that rule of sure testimony in Scripture which is by 'two witnesses' (Deut. 17:6; Matt. 18:16). How this is effected we do not know, any more than we understand the movement of the Spirit in others of his ways within us, for 'the wind blows where it wants, and you hear the sound thereof, but cannot tell whence it comes, and where it goes' (John 3:8).

Kevan went on, by reference to 'Abba, Father', in part quoting Alexander Maclaren, to help and encourage those who think they do not enjoy 'the kind of "feelings" which they thought this passage required':

The essence of the conviction which is lodged in the human spirit by the testimony of the Spirit of God 'is not primarily directed to our relation or feelings to God, but to a far grander thing than that – to God's feelings and relation to us... And so the *substance* of the Spirit's evidence is the direct conviction, based on the revelation of God's infinite love and fatherhood in Christ the Son, that God is my Father;

---

[1] Packer: *Keep* pp76-79. In light of this, I cannot fathom how Packer could speak so highly of the Puritan view of the witness of the Spirit (Packer: 'The Witness of the Spirit in Puritan Thought' pp235-250).

from which direct conviction I come to the conclusion, the inference, the second thought: "Then I may trust that I am his son. But why? Because of anything in me? No: because of him"...'

In this 'joint-witness' of the Holy Spirit with our own spirit we have the foundation of the Christian doctrine of assurance... 'Assurance', in the evangelical sense, is not the result of reason but the gift of grace. *It is the fruit, not of argument, but of inward testimony.*[2] Our filial confidence therefore is not a delusion... (1 John 3:24; 4:15)... 'Spirit, breathing from above,/ Thou hast *taught* me it is so'.[3]

Charles Wesley:

> *Spirit of faith, come down,*
> *Reveal the things of God,*
> *And make to us salvation known,*
> *And witness with the blood.*
>
> *No man can truly say*
> *That Jesus is the Lord,*
> *Unless thou take the veil away,*
> *And breathe the living word.*
>
> *Then, only then, we feel*
> *Our interest in his blood,*
> *And cry with joy unspeakable,*
> *'Thou art my Lord, my God!'*
>
> *O that the world might know*
> *The all-atoning Lamb!*
> *Spirit of faith, descend and show*
> *The virtue of his name;*
>
> *Inspire the living faith,*
> *Which whosoe'er receives,*
> *The witness in himself he has*
> *And savingly believes.*[4]

George Whitefield:

Christ came not only to save us from the guilt, but from the power of sin. Until he has done this, however... we can have no assurance or well-grounded hope that he has saved us. For it is by receiving his

---

[2] Emphasis mine.

[3] Kevan pp69-71, emphasis original except where stated.

[4] *Gospel Hymns* 363, altered.

blessed Spirit into our hearts, and feeling him witnessing with our spirits that we are the sons of God, that we can be certified of our being sealed to the day of redemption. This is a great mystery, but I speak of Christ and the new birth. Marvel not at my asking you what you think of Christ being formed within you... for as in Adam we all have spiritually died, so all that are effectually saved by Christ, must in Christ be made spiritually alive... Examine yourselves therefore... whether you are in the faith. Prove yourselves, and think that it is not sufficient to say in your creed: 'I believe in Jesus Christ'. Many say so, who do not believe, who are reprobates, and are still in a state of death. You take God's name in vain when you call him Father, and your prayers are turned into sin, unless you believe in Christ, so as to have your life hid with him in God, and to receive life and nourishment from him, as branches do from the vine.

I know, indeed, the men of this generation deny there is any such thing as feeling Christ within them, but... the apostle prays that the Ephesians may abound in all knowledge and spiritual understanding; or, as it might be rendered, spiritual sensation... For there is a spiritual as well as a corporeal feeling, and though this is not communicated to us in a sensible [externally explained] manner, as outward objects affect our senses, yet it is as real as any sensible or visible sensation, and may be as truly felt and discerned by the soul as any impression from without can be felt by the body. All who are born again of God know that I lie not.

In support of his claim, Whitefield cited Naaman cured of his leprosy, the woman cured of her haemorrhage: they both felt it, did they not? He went on:

So surely you may feel, O believer, when Jesus Christ dwells within your heart. I pray God to make you all know and feel this, ere you depart hence [that is, die]. O... my heart is enlarged towards you. I trust I feel something of that hidden but powerful presence of Christ, while I am preaching to you. Indeed, it is sweet, it is exceedingly comfortable. All the harm I wish you[5] who, without cause, are my enemies is that you felt the like.[6]

In another sermon, Whitefield issued a rebuke which needs to be taken very seriously in our dry day:

---

[5] Whitefield was being ironical.
[6] Sermon on 'What do you think of Christ?' (Matt. 22:42) in Whitefield pp291-292.

We... shall receive the Holy Ghost if we believe on the Lord Jesus with our whole hearts... All who believe in Jesus Christ... are... joined to Jesus Christ by being made partakers of the Holy Spirit. A great noise has been made of late about the word 'enthusiast',[7] and it has been cast upon the preachers of the gospel as a term of reproach. But every Christian, in the proper sense of the word, must be an enthusiast – that is, [he] must be inspired [breathed-into] of God, or have God, by his Spirit, in him... Yet, Christians must have their names cast out as evil, and ministers, in particular, must be looked upon as deceivers of the people, for affirming that we must be really united to God by receiving the Holy Ghost!... I will not say [that] all our letter-learned preachers deny this doctrine in express words, but, however, they do, in effect, [deny it], for they talk professedly against inward feelings, and say we may have God's Spirit without feeling it – which is, in reality, to deny the thing itself. And had I a mind to hinder the progress of the gospel, and to establish the kingdom of darkness, I would go about telling people [that] they might have the Spirit of God and yet not feel it.[8]

Ralph Erskine preached two sermons on the subject of 'the witness of the Spirit',[9] in which he said:

It is not a fluctuating opinion, but an internal testimony, and an internal sensation of what God testifies and speaks; namely, peace and salvation, in and through his Son, Jesus Christ... (John 15:26; 16:14; Eph. 1:13; Rom. 8:16; 2 Tim. 1:12)... The Spirit [gives] his own immediate testimony... (Rom. 8:16)... by shedding abroad the love of God upon the heart in a soul-ravishing way... It is not said 'the Spirit' but 'the Spirit himself'... The Spirit himself does it, says Paul... The Spirit applies [promises] to particular souls... The Spirit is promised to take of the things of Christ and show them to his people... Sanctification may lie dark, and yet the Spirit... may witness within. As in a dark day, a man may conclude the sun is up though he cannot see it, so a man, acting [exercising] faith on the blood of Christ, may conclude his sanctity, *though he cannot see his own sanctification; and the not drawing of this conclusion is the occasion of many fears, doubts and disquietments [anxieties] in the souls of believers...* The

---

[7] I fear something of the sort is being thought in some circles today.

[8] 'The Privilege of All Believers' in Whitefield p433.

[9] 'The Believer's Internal Witness: The Certain Evidence of True Faith', in Erskine pp29-74, a reprint of the volumes edited by Septimus Sears, emphasis mine. Note Erskine's title. He did not say that sanctification is the evidence of true faith – though it is, of course – but that the witness of the Spirit is *the certain* evidence

witness that the believer has within himself testifies and depones[10] that the believer has a union to and interest in Christ... (Song 2:16; 6:3)... The witness that the believer has in himself attests and depones that he is a child of God... (Rom. 8:16; Gal. 3:26; John 1:12)... The witness within declares this because it witnesses that the man is a believer that has received Christ... The witness that the believer has in himself attests and depones [declares under oath] that he is free from condemnation... (Rom. 8:1; John 3:18)... The witness that the believer has in himself depones that he shall be saved eternally... The witness that the believer has in himself attests and depones that nothing can be laid to his charge... The witness that the believer has in himself attest and depones that the union between Christ and him is inseparable and indissolvable... Yet this witness does not always speak within him, but when it speaks, its deposition and testimony make one or other of these things as clear as daylight to the believer... There was never such a credible witness in the world as the believer has within him...

He that believes has the witness in himself because outward witnesses cannot clear him with any comfortable evidence; and the Lord wills that believers should have strong consolation, who have fled for refuge to lay hold upon the hope set before them. But now no means... can clear, or comfortably attests his interest in Christ, his sonship or reconciliation, unless the Spirit of Christ witnesses within him. The white of a wall can as soon make day, as ministers or outward means can give comfort or clearness to a believer, unless the Spirit of the Lord concurs with the means, and witnesses in the man's bosom...

Though faith alone justifies, yet justifying faith is not alone: it has its witness with it, even the witness of the Spirit... namely manifest sanctification as well as justification...[11] Never conclude that you have true faith unless you find, or at least have found, the witness within you giving testimony thereto. If you know nothing more or less of this witness then it is plain you know nothing of true faith,[12] for it is expressly said of all believers, weak or strong: 'He that believes on the Son of God has the witness in himself'... Hence see what is the true matter of a believer's confidence and assurance. Why, they have the witness in themselves... Hence see that the believer's doubts and fears

---

[10] Gives testimony by affidavit or deposition.

[11] While I agree that sanctification is a concomitant and consequence of justification, the witness of the Spirit is first and foremost independent of sanctification, and precedes it.

[12] As I have made clear, I am sure a true believer can be in darkness and doubt. Nevertheless, even though I think Erskine is too strong, I feel we have gone far too far the other way.

and jealousies [suspicions, doubts] are inexcusable and unwarrantable, for he has the witness in himself, and his unbelieving doubts do nothing but give the lie to God's witness that is in him.[13]

J.N.Darby on 'the witness of the Spirit':

The Spirit himself bears witness with our spirit that we are the children of God... Two things are equally precious: participation in the Spirit, as the power of life by which we are capable of enjoying God, and the relationship of children to him; and the presence and authority of the Spirit to assure us of it.

As to the first:

Our position is that of sons, our proper relationship that of children. The word 'sons' is in contrast with the position under the law, which was that of servants; it is the state of privilege in its widest extent. To say the 'child' of such a one implies the intimacy and reality of the relationship.

Darby spoke of 'two operations of the Spirit':

The communication of assurance of being children with all its glorious consequences; and his work of sympathy and grace in connection with the sorrows and infirmities in which the child is found here below.

As for 'the first point' – 'that the Spirit himself bears witness with our spirit that we are the children of the family of God' – in a highly preceptive statement, Darby rightly distinguished the twofold witness within the believer:

The Holy Ghost (acting in us...) has produced the affections of a child, and, by the affections, the consciousness of being a child of God, so he does not separate himself from this, but, by his powerful presence, he bears witness himself that we are children. We have this testimony in our hearts in our relationship with God, but the Holy Ghost himself, as distinct from us, bears this testimony to us in whom he dwells. The true freed Christian knows that his heart recognises God as Father, but he also knows that the Holy Ghost himself bears his testimony to him

---

[13] Sears, very much in line with his hesitation over Erskine's freeness in offering Christ to sinners (see my *Septimus*), added notes to strengthen the need for true faith and sanctification. Yes, indeed, but Erskine's freeness when speaking of assurance must not be lost!

[the believer]. That which is founded on the word is realised and verified in the heart.

Darby went on to speak of the way the witness of the Spirit enables the believer to come through the many sorrows and trials which befall him, and to long for the glory to come. I forbear to quote at length, but here is a sample:

The Spirit, who makes us know that we are children and heirs of glory, teaches us by the same means to understand all the misery of the creature... Thus also we wait for the adoption, that is, the redemption of the body. For as to possession of the full result, it is in hope [confident expectation – DG] that we are saved; so that meanwhile we groan, as well as understand, according to the Spirit and our new disposition,[14] that all creation groans... Here... also the operation of the Holy Ghost has its place, as well as bearing witness that we are children and heirs of God with Christ.[15]

John Stott, posing the question: 'Precisely how is the Spirit's witness borne?', delineated the answer in four parts. While I do not altogether agree with Stott here, there is enough for me to quote him:

First, the Spirit leads us into holiness (Rom. 8:13-14) ([note] the conjunction 'because').[16] Secondly, in our relationship to God he replaces fear with freedom (Rom. 8:15). Thirdly, in our prayers he prompts us to call God 'Father' (Rom. 8:15-16). Fourthly, he is the firstfruits of our heavenly inheritance (Rom. 8:17,23). Thus radical holiness, fearless freedom, filial prayerfulness and the hope of glory are four characteristics of the children of God who are indwelt and led

---

[14] Darby had 'nature'.

[15] Darby pp200-204.

[16] This is not what Paul is saying. Rather, a man can only live according to the Spirit if he has the Spirit. It is true, of course, that a man who has the Spirit will not live according to the flesh, but will live according to the Spirit, and that he is obliged to do so, but Paul is here dealing with, and contrasting, the two states of man: flesh and Spirit. Stott was making sanctification a primary aspect of assurance, but this is *not* what the apostle is saying in verses 13-14.

by the Spirit of God.[17] It is by these evidences that he witnesses to us that we are God's children.[18]

In particular, how does the Spirit bear witness with us? Stott noted the word in question – *symmartyreō* – commenting:

Normally *syn* is translated 'together with', in which case there would be two witnesses here, the Holy Spirit confirming and endorsing our own spirit's consciousness of God's Fatherhood... This would be readily understandable, since the Old Testament required two witnesses to establish a testimony (Deut. 9:15). On the other hand, is it really possible in experience to distinguish between the Holy Spirit and our human spirit? More important, would not these two witnesses be inappropriately matched?... In this case the prefix *syn* is simply intensive, and Paul meant that the Holy Spirit bears a strong inward witness *to* our spirit that we are God's children.

Stott rightly linked this with Romans 5:5.[19]

Terris Neuman, commenting on Galatians 3:1-5:

The Galatian Christians had received the Spirit at the time of their conversion to Christ. This is supported by the use of the participle... 'having started' [Gal. 3:3]... As Dunn says, it 'cannot refer to anything other than the moment of becoming a Christian'.[20] The reception of the Spirit is the beginning of the Christian life. This adverbial participle does not point to anything consequent to the beginning of the believer's new life, 'but rather takes it for granted that the beginning of the Christian life and the reception of the Spirit are coterminous [having the same boundaries or extent in space, time, or meaning]'.[21]

Neuman went on to quote Dunn further:

James Dunn says the distinctive mark of the Christian is experience of the Spirit, but not merely the experience of the Spirit... Rather, 'the

---

[17] Which is all believers. Stott was not saying that some believers are indwelt by the Spirit, and others not. See John 14:16-17,23; Rom. 8:9,11; 1 Cor. 3:16; 6:19; 2 Cor. 6:16; Gal. 4:6; 2 Tim. 1:14; 1 John 4:13.
[18] Stott p230.
[19] Stott p234.
[20] Dunn: *Baptism* p108.
[21] Neuman p60, quoting Longenecker p103.

distinctive mark of the Christian is experience of the Spirit *as the life of Christ*.[22]

Douglas Moo:

If some Christians err in basing their assurance on feelings alone, many others err in basing it on facts and arguments alone. Indeed, what Paul says here [Rom. 8:15] calls into question whether one can have a genuine experience of God's spirit of adoption without its affecting the emotions... The Holy Spirit is not only instrumental in *making* us God's children; he also makes us *aware* that we are God's children.[23]

I would strengthen Moo. Being unaware that one is converted more than 'calls [the experience] into question'. I fail to see how a sinner can be converted and it not 'affect the emotions'. Listen to the retort of the blind man to the carping Pharisees: 'One thing I do know. I was blind but now I see!' (John 9:25). I, for one, can feel the emotion in his words. An emotion-less faith is a Sandemanian faith, and, therefore, not saving.

Robert Hawker:

Reader, let you and me learn to rightly value our privileges! Blessed be God, we are not come to the mount that might be touched, and that burned with fire, and blackness, and darkness, and tempest! Oh, what an awful dispensation, to shadow forth the terror, and dread, with which the broken law of God stood over the alarmed conscience of the trembling, guilty soul! Well might it be called the ministration of death, for it denounced everlasting indignation and wrath, tribulation and anguish, to every soul of man that does evil. Reader, what a mercy is it, that the poor sinner is come not to mount Sinai, but to mount Zion; not to the law to condemn, but to the gospel to save; even to Jesus the Mediator of the new covenant, and to the blood of sprinkling, that speaks better things than that of Abel. Lord, take away every remaining veil, of darkness and unbelief. Cause my soul, with open face, to behold as in a glass the glory of the Lord! Cause my soul to be changed into the same image, from glory to glory, even as by the Spirit of the Lord. And... almighty Spirit, grant me freedom of access to the mercy seat of my God in Christ. For where you, Lord, are, there is liberty. Oh, for liberty to pray, to plead, to wrestle with my God in prayer, in the blood, obedience, and death, of our Lord Jesus Christ.

---

[22] Dunn: *Jesus* p323 (Neuman p65, emphasis mine).
[23] Moo pp502-503, emphasis his.

Give me, Lord, that sweet spirit of adoption, that I may be no longer under a spirit of bondage, but cry: 'Abba, Father'. And, oh,... be an unceasing witness to my spirit that I am a child of God![24]

Again:

The faith of God's people is supposed by the gospel to be a life of trust, assurance, and confirmation. The prophet, ages before the coming of Christ, declared that the work of righteousness (Christ's righteousness) shall be peace; and the effect of righteousness, quietness, and assurance for ever (Isa. 32:1). And to this purport, the promise runs along with it, and keeps pace together: 'You will keep him in perfect peace whose mind is stayed on you, because he trusts in you' (Isa. 26:3). If, therefore, there remained any uncertainty in respect to the justified state of a child of God, whom God by sovereign grace has called with an holy calling, those blessed scriptures lose their power. That man cannot be said to have quietness, and assurance for ever, as an effect of his interest in, and dependence upon, the righteousness of the Lord Jesus Christ, while the shadow of a doubt remains in his mind, whether [or not] he has received pardon, mercy, and peace, in the blood of the cross, and is justified by faith, through our Lord Jesus Christ. Now the groundwork on which the child of God, truly taught of God, rests his full assurance of faith, and which keeps him, as Paul says he was kept from fainting, is the heart-felt conviction that Christ, when he stood forth the Surety of his church and people, truly, as the prophet said of him, finished the transgression, made an end of sin, made reconciliation for iniquity, and brought in an everlasting righteousness (Dan. 9:24). In all that high transaction, Christ acted as his people's Sponsor and Surety; and, therefore, not an atom of guilt, either original or actual, was left un-atoned on his people's conscience. Now then, if I, or you, or any and every child of God, whom God hath effectually called by grace, believe the record,[25] which God hath given of his dear Son – namely, that God hath given eternal life to his whole body the church, in his dear Son, and that, by virtue of the infinite value and preciousness of his righteousness and blood-shedding, they are justified from all things – how is it possible that there can be any suspense, doubt, or misgiving, on this grand assurance of the redeemed child of God's hope? Reader! Do look, again and again, at the blessed frame of mind Paul was in, and which wholly arose from this one cause. And recollect that this high privilege

---

[24] Hawker: *Commentary* on 2 Cor. 3 (studylight.org).
[25] Saving faith is more than 'believing the record'; it involves trust in Christ.

was not Paul's privilege only, but the whole church of God is equally begotten to it, and equally entitled to it, with the apostle, because it arises not from any merit, or services in Paul, but [is] the sole gift of God in Christ... As we have received mercy, we faint not.[26]

Again:

The leadings of the Spirit, and the witnessings of the Spirit, are all manifest in their daily tokens of grace,[27] the sonship and privileges of the regenerate in Christ. It is they, and they only, which have freeness of access to the throne, and to the pardon-office of Christ, and can, and do say: 'Abba, Father'. No servants, no bondsmen, no unregenerate – none but those of the family of God in Christ, who are heirs of God, and joint-heirs with Christ – can so approach, or claim such a relationship. A union with Christ is the only foundation for enjoying communion with the heirship of Christ. It is because you are sons (says the apostle elsewhere) God hath sent forth the Spirit of his Son into your hearts, crying: 'Abba, Father' (Gal. 4:6).
Reader! Pause, and contemplate the blessedness of such a state! By virtue of their adoption-character, [believers] are brought into the present enjoyment by faith, of their vast inheritance; and have a full right in Christ to the sanctified use of all temporal blessings, the privilege of all spiritual blessings, and ere long to the complete enjoyment of all eternal blessings, for they are heirs of God and joint-heirs with Christ.[28]

Again, putting his thoughts into a hymn:

> *'Tis thine, O Lord, in blessing thus,*
> *To take of Christ's and show to us,*
> *Of him, and his, impart;*
> *And thine no less the same to prove,*
> *And shed abroad the Father's love,*
> *In each renewèd heart.*

William Tyndale rightly distinguished historical faith (mere assent to the truth) and saving faith, which he called 'feeling faith':

The elect [who have been converted] [are those] in whose hearts God has written his law by his Spirit, and given them a feeling faith of the mercy that is in Christ Jesus our Lord... There are two sorts of faith:

---

[26] Hawker: *Commentary* on 2 Cor. 4 (studylight.org).
[27] Excellent – *'daily* tokens'.
[28] Hawker: *Commentary* on Rom.8 (studylight.org).

historical faith, and feeling faith... Of feeling faith, it is written: 'They shall all be taught of God' [John 6:45]; that is, God shall write it in their hearts with his Holy Spirit. And Paul also testifies: 'The Spirit bears record [witness] unto our spirit, that we are the sons of God' [Rom. 8:16]. And this faith is no opinion, but a sure feeling, and therefore is ever fruitful. Neither does it hang on the honesty of the preacher, but of the power of God, and of the Spirit... If I have no other feeling in my faith than because a man says [something or other], then is my faith faithless and fruitless... Christ's elect church is the whole multitude of all repenting sinners that believe in Christ, and put all their trust and confidence in the mercy of God, feeling in their hearts that God for Christ's sake loves them, and will be, or rather is, merciful unto them, and forgives them their sins of which they repent; and that he forgives all the motions unto sin, of which they fear lest they should be drawn into sin again.[29]

Tyndale spoke of those who, believing in Christ, are walking 'in the open light and feeling' and who have the 'inward feeling that the Spirit of God' gives, warning against those who 'believe' without 'feeling the mercy that is in Christ', 'who serve God with works, [and] have no feeling'.[30] And what is 'feeling' if not assurance?

And now C.H.Spurgeon, preaching on Ephesians 1:13. Although he didn't get it all right, Spurgeon said a great many important things, and said them in his usual pithy and telling way:

Many sincerely seeking souls are in great trouble because they have not yet attained to an assurance of their interest in Christ Jesus... And herein they pierce themselves through with many sorrows. Perhaps they will not fall into this error again if they get a right understanding of the text before us... Paul here explains the process by which sealing – the sealing of assurance – is obtained. There are three steps by which the hallowed elevation is reached. The first is hearing – they heard first the preaching of the word. The second is believing. And then, thirdly, 'after that you believed, you were sealed with the Holy Spirit of promise'...
Sealing, which is another name for assurance, for the witness of the Holy Spirit with our spirit – that we are born of God, is evidently distinct from faith. Please observe that – for the text says: 'After that you believed, you were sealed with the Holy Spirit of promise'.

---

[29] Tyndale pp13,50-52.
[30] Tyndale pp149,69,114,182.

Believing, then, is not this sealing. And assurance, although it is akin to believing, is not believing. There is a distinction between the two things. I want you to notice the distinction. In faith the mind is active. The text uses verbs which imply action – 'you trusted', 'you believed'. But when it comes to sealing it uses quite another verb – 'you were sealed'. I am active in believing – I am passive when the Holy Spirit seals me. The witness of the Spirit is something which I receive, but faith is something which I exercise as well as receive. In faith my mind does something – in being sealed my faith receives something. If I may say so, faith writes out the document – there she labours – but the Holy Spirit stamps the seal himself and there is no hand wanted there except his own. He stamps his own impression to make the document valid. Notice the difference between the activeness and the passiveness.
Then, again, man is commanded to believe in Scripture in many places – but he never was commanded to be sealed. Faith is a duty as well as a privilege, but assurance a privilege only. I never find any man exhorted to get the sealing of the Spirit...[31] I know of no command. It is a gift, a priceless gift and, unlike faith, it does not constitute a... command. Again, we read in Scripture that men are saved by faith and live by faith, but neither salvation nor living are ever imputed to sealing or to assurance. We are not saved by assurance – we do not even live by assurance. The vital principle is couched in faith. That is the shell which holds the kernel of the inner spiritual life. I may be saved though I never had assurance. But even if I fancied I had assurance, I could not be saved if I had not faith. To faith we say salvation is promised, but to assurance such a promise is not given.

Unfortunately, Spurgeon then built much – far too much – on the unwarranted insertion of 'after'. Nevertheless, having set out a very important principle – one which I have deliberately omitted, and to which I will return – Spurgeon went on:

This assurance, like faith, is the work of the Spirit of God. 'You were sealed with the Holy Spirit of promise'. He does this in various ways. Sometimes we get the seal of the Spirit through experience. We know that God is true because we have proved him. Sometimes this comes through the hearing of the word – as we listen our faith is confirmed. But there is doubtless, besides this, a special and supernatural work of the Holy Spirit whereby men are assured that they are born of God.

---

[31] This is one of those places where Spurgeon went beyond Scripture when he said: 'I believe that every Christian should pray for it and seek it, but I know of no command'. Would: 'I do believe; help me overcome my unbelief!' (Mark 9:24) justify his claim?

You will observe in one place the apostle says: 'The Spirit also bears witness with our spirit, that we are born of God', so that there are two witnesses – first, our spirit bears witness, that is, by evidences. I look at my faith and see myself depending upon Christ and then I know, because I love the brethren and for other reasons, that I am born of God.

Then there comes over and above the witness of evidence, faith and feeling – the Spirit himself bearing witness with our spirit.[32] Have you not felt it? I cannot describe this to you, but you who have felt it know it. Did you not the other day feel a heavenly calm as you meditated upon your state and condition in Christ? You wondered where it came from. It was not the result of protracted devotion but it stole over you – you knew not how it was – you were bathed in it as in sunlight and you rejoiced exceedingly. You rejoiced in Christ – that was your basis of confidence, and that confidence came through the Spirit bearing witness with your spirit. This has occurred sometimes in the midst of sharp conflicts just when dark despair seemed ready to overwhelm you. You may have enjoyed this comfort under peculiar trials and losses of friends and you may expect to have it when you come to die. Then, if ever in your life, you should be able to say: 'I will fear no evil, for you are with me (in a special sense); you are with me'. The Holy Spirit, then, must give it [the witness, the seal] to us...[33] And so to conclude, this is desirable to the highest degree, for it is the earnest of the inheritance. It is a part of heaven on earth to get an assurance worked by the Spirit!

I return to that important section I deliberately omitted:

Observe in the next place... that assurance is to be found where faith was found. Do observe those two words, 'in whom' – 'in whom you also trusted' – 'in whom you were sealed'. So that as I get my faith out of Christ, so I must get my assurance out of Christ. The virtual means of my faith is Christ himself and the virtual means of my assurance must be the same. As I think of what he did for me, I believe in him. As I continue to meditate upon that same thing, I have assurance of interest in him. You must feed upon the flesh and blood of Christ if you would grow into strong men in Christ Jesus. A touch of Christ will heal you from all disease – but you must hold him fast if you would enjoy spiritual health perpetually. To believe in Christ will save you

---

[32] In saying this, Spurgeon mistakenly put evidences before the witness of the Spirit.

[33] Spurgeon had: 'And we must wait upon him to set his seal'. I see no biblical justification for this.

from hell. To be assured of your interest in Christ will give you a heaven upon earth! Do not be content with faith – be thankful for it, rejoice in it – but ask to have more. And when you want to have more, go to Christ for it – the same fountain which first quenched your thirst must be that which shall quench it till you are taken up to drink of the river of life which flows through the midst of paradise – which is no other than the presence of Christ as a refreshment to his people.[34]

Charitie Bancroft:

Before the throne of God above
I have a strong, a perfect plea.
A great High Priest whose name is Love
Who ever lives and pleads for me.

My name is graven on his hands,
My name is written on his heart.
I know that, while in heaven he stands,
No tongue can bid me thence depart.

When Satan tempts me to despair
And tells me of the guilt within,
Upward I look, and see him there
Who made an end of all my sin.

Because the sinless Saviour died
My sinful soul is counted free;
For God the just is satisfied
To look on him and pardon me.

Behold him there! the risen Lamb!
My perfect, spotless righteousness,
The great unchangeable I AM,
The King of glory and of grace,

One with himself I cannot die.
My soul is purchased by his blood,
My life is hid with Christ on high,
With Christ my Saviour and my God.

Notice that! When Satan tempts me to despair, I do not look within or at others; I look up to Christ. As Paul thundered:

---

[34] Sermon number 592.

Who will bring any charge against those whom God has chosen? It is God who justifies. Who is he that condemns? Christ Jesus, who died – more than that, who was raised to life – is at the right hand of God and is also interceding for us (Rom. 8:33-34).[35]

John Newton:

> *What think ye of Christ? is the test*
> *To try both your state and your scheme;*
> *You cannot be right in the rest,*
> *Unless you think rightly of him.*
> *As Jesus appears in your view,*
> *As he is beloved or not;*
> *So God is disposed to you,*
> *And mercy or wrath are your lot.*
>
> *Some take him a creature to be,*
> *A man, or an angel at most;*
> *Sure these have not feelings like me,*
> *Nor know themselves wretched and lost:*
> *So guilty, so helpless, am I,*
> *I dare not confide in his blood,*
> *Nor on his protection rely,*
> *Unless I were sure he is God.*
>
> *If asked what of Jesus I think?*
> *Though still my best thoughts are but poor;*
> *I say, he's my meat and my drink,*
> *My life, and my strength, and my store,*
> *My Shepherd, my Husband, my Friend,*
> *My Saviour from sin and from thrall;*
> *My hope from beginning to end,*
> *My Portion, my Lord, and my All.*

And although the poetry is not up to much (even allowing for translation), there's no mistaking Daniel Rowland's theology:

> *Come! Praise the King of heaven above.*
> *His grace to me is sealed!*
> *He gave his Son, no greater gift;*
> *I know whom I have trusted.*

---

[35] The NIV is excellent here, having not inserted 'It is' before 'Christ'

I doubted long his loving grace,
The gospel[36] I rejected;
Illumination now has come;
I know whom I have trusted.

Through Christ I'm justified by faith,
To this his Spirit's witnessed;
Henceforth who dares condemn my soul?
I know whom I have trusted.

I see by faith that now I live,
God's earnest has been granted;
Th'inheritance will duly come;
I know whom I have trusted.

He who began this blessed work
Its progress also charted,
Till Canaan's rest is mine for aye;
I know whom I have trusted.[37]

---

[36] Rowland had 'religion'.
[37] Evans p253.

Appendix 3

1 John

Many think that John, in his first letter, is giving believers a series of tests by which they can examine themselves, and so come to assurance. Indeed, some go so far as to think John is actually insisting on such tests for assurance. Listen to Robert A.Morey:

John constantly challenges our assurance by saying: 'Hereby we know him if...'. He *demands* that we 'prove' or 'test' our assurance of salvation. This proof is obtained by self-examination. John *calls upon us* to examine our lives to see if God has truly given us a new heart.[1]

This is a serious misreading of the apostle.

John had several purposes in writing his letter. First, like other New Testament writers, he was tackling false teachers; in his case, the Gnostics. Linked with his first aim, he was confronting mere professors, telling them in no uncertain terms that a true conversion reveals itself in observable change, in a Christ-like life. And, thirdly, he wanted to comfort and reassure doubting believers, believers who had lost their assurance and subsequent joy. It is John's third purpose which concerns us here.

John was writing to doubting believers. That much is clear. But why were they doubting? Throughout the New Testament, we see how false teachers (Judaisers, Gnostics, whatever) and their teaching brought the early believers into bondage and sadness – not least in taking them to the law, with the consequent loss of their assurance. So here. John wrote his letter to help believers regain their sense of assurance after they had lost it through being brought into bondage through the Gnostics. And he did it by taking them back to where they had left the road.

He was doing something similar to Paul, writing to the Galatians: 'What has happened to all your joy?' he asked them (Gal. 4:15). In their case, they had lost it through listening to the Judaisers, the law teachers. And the apostle set about restoring their

---

[1] Morey, emphasis mine.

137

joy and sense of liberty by instructing the Galatians, challenging them, and taking them back to the beginning, to where they had left the track (Gal. 2:16 – 3:5). Had they not been justified in Christ? Had they not received the gift of the Spirit? Of course they had! But how had they been justified and received the Spirit? By the law? They had not! Very well then. As they had begun, so they should continue. Assurance, adoption, sanctification, liberty, glory... all of it comes through Christ and not by the law.[2]

The principle is plain: if believers try to find assurance by their sanctification under the law, they will come into bondage and sadness through their inevitable failure to reach the standard. And the remedy is always the same: they must go back to the root of their joy in salvation; namely, Christ.

All this applies to John's letter. False teaching brings believers into doubt. As John's closing remarks make clear:

I write these things to you who believe in the name of the Son of God so that you may know that you have eternal life. This is the confidence we have in approaching God: that if we ask anything according to his will, he hears us. And if we know that he hears us – whatever we ask – we know that we have what we asked of him... The one who was born of God keeps him safe, and the evil one cannot harm him. We know that we are children of God, and that the whole world is under the control of the evil one. We know also that the Son of God has come and has given us understanding, so that we may know him who is true. And we are in him who is true – even in his Son Jesus Christ. He is the true God and eternal life. Dear children, keep yourselves from idols (1 John 5:13-15,18-21).

Here we have both the cure for doubt, and its preventative: 'Dear children, keep yourselves from idols'. Keep to Christ!

And do not miss John's confidence: 'We know'! No lack of assurance on John's part here! 'We know also...'. No lack of assurance on John's part here! 'We know also that the Son of God has come and has given us understanding, so that we may know him who is true. And we are in him...'. No lack of assurance on John's part here!

Nor here:

---

[2] For the full argument, see my *Christ*; *Galatians*.

But you have an anointing from the Holy One, and all of you know the truth. I do not write to you because you do not know the truth, but because you do know it and because no lie comes from the truth... We know that when he appears, we shall be like him, for we shall see him as he is... You know that he appeared so that he might take away our sins... We know that we have passed from death to life, because we love our brothers... We know what love is: Jesus Christ laid down his life for us... Those who obey his commands live in him, and he in them. And this is how we know that he lives in us: we know it by the Spirit he gave us... We know that we live in him and he in us, because he has given us of his Spirit... We know and rely on the love God has for us... This is how we know that we love the children of God: by loving God and carrying out his commands... (1 John 2:20-21; 3:2,5,14,16,24; 4:13,16; 5:2).

Yes, I realise that one or two of these statements are generally taken to be tests, tests which believers should apply to themselves to give them assurance. While there is an element of truth in this, it must be carefully nuanced. To make sanctification the way of assurance is to misread the apostle, with serious consequences.

John, we must not forget, has his own idiosyncratic way of writing; he puts things 'back to front!'[3] Every writer has his own peculiar way of expressing things, of course. As a man can be recognised by his handwriting, so he can by the way he strings his words together: every writer has his own voice.[4] 1 John 5:1 is typical of the striking way the apostle likes to put things: 'Everyone who believes that Jesus is the Christ is born of God'. John was not saying that regeneration follows faith; rather, faith is the evidence of prior regeneration. But, as I say, the apostle likes putting things back to front.

Take, for instance: 'You know that everyone who does what is right has been born of [God]' (1 John 2:29). This does not mean that the practice of righteousness leads to, produces regeneration;

---

[3] Compare 'the man said' with 'said the man'.
[4] Paul had. John had. I have. I have been told that people can hear me speaking as they read my books. Quite! See Stanley Baldwin's letter to Winston Churchill on reading the latter's first volume on the life of Marlborough (Gilbert pp80,104). See Lloyd-Jones: *Gospel* pp13-14. '[Thomas] Carlyle... contrived to get the sound of his own spoken voice into his writings' (Abrams p948).

rather, the practice of righteousness is the proof, the evidence, the demonstration, of the fact that a sinner has been regenerated.

'He who does what is right is righteous' (1 John 3:7); that is, sanctification is a sure sign of justification, not the cause of it.

'This is how we know who the children of God are and who the children of the devil are: anyone who does not do what is right is not a child of God; nor is anyone who does not love his brother' (1 John 3:10). John is not saying that sanctification produces justification. He is not saying that by his godliness a man becomes a child of God. No! But because a man is a child of God, he will live a godly life. It is just the apostle's own way of expressing himself.

'Every spirit that acknowledges that Jesus Christ has come in the flesh is from God' (1 John 4:2); that is, spiritual, believing, confession of the incarnation of Christ is evidence – not the cause – of regeneration, the evidence of a man being 'of God'.

'Everyone who loves is born of God' (1 John 4:7, NKJV); spiritual love is an evidence of regeneration – not that regeneration is produced by it: 'Everyone who loves has been born of God and knows God' (1 John 4:7, NIV).

Yet in all these passages, at first glance John seems to be saying the opposite. It's simply the striking way he puts things; regeneration comes first!

Take another of John's statements – this time where he expresses himself the 'right way round':

No one who is born of God will continue to sin, because God's seed remains in him; he cannot go on sinning, because he has been born of God... Everyone born of God overcomes the world... We know that anyone born of God does not continue to sin (1 John 3:9; 5:4,18).

What I am saying is this: we can read John's words as tests by which we have to probe ourselves to gain assurance. The right way to read him, however, is to realise he was giving *encouragements* to his readers who had lost their assurance, writing in order to reassure them. John was sure about his readers; he wants them to be sure! Applying it to ourselves: John's 'tests', far from being hoops through which believers have to jump in order to be assured, *are encouragements to **reassure** believers who have lost their joy.* Stibbs and Packer, having pointed out that the early believers generally did not lack assurance, and, therefore, the New Testament never discusses it, then went on to say:

The nearest thing to such a discussion is the first letter of John, which was written partly to *re*assure Christians whose prior assurance had been shaken by false teachers telling them that they were really still in darkness; but this is a different issue from that of leading into assurance Christians who have never had it.[5]

We must take a firm grip on this: John is *not* giving a series of tests by which believers can and should test themselves to come to assurance.

That being said, John's assurances, of course, are only assurances to those who are living in the way he delineates. In other words, although I do not think John's words should be used to harrow believers – rather, they should be used as reassurances for true believers – they are to be so used only by those who are demonstrating the marks of sanctification he sets out. John was not encouraging so-called 'carnal Christians' to live as they want. Not at all! But he was reassuring true believers who were living for Christ (or, at the very least, were honestly seeking to glorify Christ by obeying his commands), and so he must be read. But whatever we take from John, it is quite wrong to think that he was telling the saints that their sanctification was the source of their assurance.

Not at all! John was clear on the witness of the Spirit as the primary source of assurance: 'anointing' seems to be his favourite word to describe it. Indeed, no New Testament writer is clearer and stronger and more emphatic (repeatedly so) upon the Spirit's anointing, the gift of the Spirit, the witness of the Spirit for every believer:

You have an anointing from the Holy One, and all of you know the truth. I do not write to you because you do not know the truth, but because you do know it and because no lie comes from the truth... As for you, the anointing you received from him remains in you, and you do not need anyone to teach you. But as his anointing teaches you about all things and as that anointing is real, not counterfeit – just as it has taught you, remain in him (1 John 2:20-27).

---

[5] Stibbs and Packer p87, emphasis theirs.

This is how we know that he lives in us: we know it by the Spirit he gave us (1 John 3:24).
We know that we live in him and he in us, because he has given us of his Spirit (1 John 4:13).
It is the Spirit who testifies, because the Spirit is the truth... We accept man's testimony, but God's testimony is greater because it is the testimony of God, which he has given about his Son. Anyone who believes in the Son of God has this testimony in his heart. Anyone who does not believe God has made him out to be a liar, because he has not believed the testimony God has given about his Son. And this is the testimony: God has given us eternal life, and this life is in his Son (1 John 5:6,9-11).

It is this that puts John's 'tests' in their proper light:

We know that we have come to know [Christ] if we obey his commands. The man who says: 'I know him', but does not do what he commands is a liar, and the truth is not in him. But if anyone obeys his word, God's love is truly made complete in him. This is how we know we are in him: Whoever claims to live in him must walk as Jesus did... Anyone who claims to be in the light but hates his brother is still in the darkness. Whoever loves his brother lives in the light, and there is nothing in him to make him stumble. But whoever hates his brother is in the darkness and walks around in the darkness; he does not know where he is going, because the darkness has blinded him... Do not love the world or anything in the world. If anyone loves the world, the love of the Father is not in him. For everything in the world – the cravings of sinful man, the lust of his eyes and the boasting of what he has and does – comes not from the Father but from the world... Dear children, this is the last hour; and as you have heard that the antichrist is coming, even now many antichrists have come. This is how we know it is the last hour. They went out from us, but they did not really belong to us. For if they had belonged to us, they would have remained with us; but their going showed that none of them belonged to us (1 John 2:3-6,9-11,15-19).
How great is the love the Father has lavished on us, that we should be called children of God! And that is what we are! The reason the world does not know us is that it did not know him. Dear friends, now we are children of God, and what we will be has not yet been made known. But we know that when he appears, we shall be like him, for we shall see him as he is. Everyone who has this hope in him purifies himself, just as he is pure. Everyone who sins breaks the law; in fact, sin is lawlessness. But you know that he appeared so that he might take away our sins. And in him is no sin. No one who lives in him keeps on

sinning. No one who continues to sin has either seen him or known him. Dear children, do not let anyone lead you astray. He who does what is right is righteous, just as he is righteous. He who does what is sinful is of the devil, because the devil has been sinning from the beginning. The reason the Son of God appeared was to destroy the devil's work. No one who is born of God will continue to sin, because God's seed remains in him; he cannot go on sinning, because he has been born of God. This is how we know who the children of God are and who the children of the devil are: Anyone who does not do what is right is not a child of God; nor is anyone who does not love his brother (1 John 3:1-10).

This is the message you heard from the beginning: We should love one another... We know that we have passed from death to life, because we love our brothers. Anyone who does not love remains in death. Anyone who hates his brother is a murderer, and you know that no murderer has eternal life in him. This is how we know what love is: Jesus Christ laid down his life for us. And we ought to lay down our lives for our brothers. If anyone has material possessions and sees his brother in need but has no pity on him, how can the love of God be in him? Dear children, let us not love with words or tongue but with actions and in truth. This then is how we know that we belong to the truth, and how we set our hearts at rest in his presence whenever our hearts condemn us. For God is greater than our hearts, and he knows everything. Dear friends, if our hearts do not condemn us, we have confidence before God, and receive from him anything we ask, because we obey his commands and do what pleases him. And this is his command: to believe in the name of his Son, Jesus Christ, and to love one another as he commanded us. Those who obey his commands live in him, and he in them. And this is how we know that he lives in us: we know it by the Spirit he gave us (1 John 3:11-24).

John was saying all this to believers, believers who, of course, had been assured by the witness (anointing) of the Spirit, but believers, who, sadly, had lost their assurance as a result of false teaching. The false teachers had taken the believers' eyes off Christ, and that had led them into all sorts of difficulty (and, I am sure, sadness for John). As he made clear right from the start: 'We write this to make our [or your] joy complete' (1 John 1:4). And, coming to the end of his letter, he could say: 'I write these things to you who believe in the name of the Son of God so that you may know that you have eternal life' (1 John 5:13). 'Dear children, keep yourselves from idols' (1 John 5:21). Keep hold of Christ!

Nor must we forget what he had already said:

This then is how we know that we belong to the truth, and how we set
our hearts at rest in his presence whenever our hearts condemn us. For
God is greater than our hearts, and he knows everything (1 John 3:19-
20).

John's use of 'to know', *ginōskō* and *eidō* (*oida*), merits careful and
detailed study. The words are richly nuanced.[6] Lloyd-Jones got it
wrong when he claimed that John was speaking about 'what we
deduce about ourselves when we apply to our lives, and to our
experiences, the various tests which are given us in the Scriptures...
1 John 3:14'.[7] The idea of 'deduce' is quite wrong here. The thrust
of 'know' is 'experience, know directly' or 'know by reflection and
meditation' – not 'discover by deduction'. Eaton:

The 'tests of conversion' approach to 1 John is refuted entirely by
these verses [1 John 2:12-14]. John is far from wanting his 'little
children' to look to their personal character or their estimate of their
spiritual strength in order to discover whether they are converted. Any
sensitive soul who truly tries this will end up in endless introspection.
It is only the Pharisee who can examine himself and then say with
assurance: 'I thank you I am not as other men', and come away with
assurance.[8]

John assures his readers: 'Your sins are forgiven', and forgiven for
Christ's sake, his 'name' (his person and work). They have
'known' God, he tells them, they have 'overcome the evil one',
they 'are strong', and God's word 'lives' in them (1 John 2:12-14).
He has no doubt about it. And he wants them to feel it, to enjoy it,
to delight in it, for themselves. He writes to reassure them, to show
them that the false teaching they have imbibed is bankrupt, and so
nerve them to resist the Gnostics. There's not the slightest
suggestion that he wants to make his readers introspective. He
doesn't doubt the reality of their conversion: to make them doubt it
is the last thing in his mind! Rather, he wants to put backbone and
joy into them by reassuring them. The heretics and their false
teaching had unsettled his readers, had robbed them of their

---

[6] See Thayer.
[7] Lloyd-Jones *Sons* p303; see Eaton *1,2,3 John* pp20-25.
[8] Eaton: *1,2,3 John* pp62-63.

assurance and happiness. John wants to bring the believers back to the basics so that they might recover their assurance – and in this way stand up to the heretics, and get rid of them and their false teaching with its inevitable misery and bondage. He not only points the believers to the evidence of their godliness to assure them, but he calls for their continuance in the faith in order to assure other believers that they are truly converted (1 John 1:6; 2:4-6; 4:20). As he asserts, true believers have the Spirit (1 John 4:13), and it shows (1 John 3:24; 4:12):

We know that we have passed from death to life, because we love our brothers. Anyone who does not love remains in death. Anyone who hates his brother is a murderer, and you know that no murderer has eternal life in him. This is how we know what love is: Jesus Christ laid down his life for us. And we ought to lay down our lives for our brothers. If anyone has material possessions and sees his brother in need but has no pity on him, how can the love of God be in him? Dear children, let us not love with words or tongue but with actions and in truth. This then is how we know that we belong to the truth, and how we set our hearts at rest in his presence whenever our hearts condemn us. For God is greater than our hearts, and he knows everything. Dear friends, if our hearts do not condemn us, we have confidence before God and receive from him anything we ask, because we obey his commands and do what pleases him. And this is his command: to believe in the name of his Son, Jesus Christ, and to love one another as he commanded us. Those who obey his commands live in him, and he in them. And this is how we know that he lives in us: we know it by the Spirit he gave us (1 John 3:14-24).

As a result, John's 'tests' need careful handling. Just as with medicine for the body, so with medicine for the soul. A physician prescribes medicine A for condition X, and medicine B for condition Y. If I have condition X, and I take medicine B, it will do me no good; it might make the disease worse and do me serious harm; it might even prove fatal. So with medicine for the soul. If you are a Gnostic in any shape or form, reader, pay serious attention to John's words. You are in error; give up your error and come to Christ as he is revealed in the New Testament. If you are one of those so-called 'carnal Christians', read John's warnings, and take them home to yourself: be converted! If you are a doubting believer, doubting because you have listened to legal preachers, Gnostics or whatever, then take a good dose of John's comforting cordial. Retrace your steps to where you left the road, get your mind and heart fixed on Christ, listen to the witness of the Spirit, and be reassured by the evidences of godliness in your life.

Alas, doubting believers can get John's teaching wrong, even turning it upside down, and so make their condition far worse. Although John's tests can be read as though he wanted believers to get anxious about themselves, and probe themselves as to the reality of their conversion, that is to *misread* him! The apostle's actual purpose, I say again, was very different. He was doing all he could to encourage and reassure such believers, and so bring them into liberty! He was doing all he could to restore them to where they were when they came into the faith.

In other words, while John's 'tests' certainly ought to strike fear into the false professor and the so-called 'carnal Christian', they ought to be a means of succour and encouragement to the sincere and true believer.

Let me put it another way. We should not view John's tests as a stiff barrier for the doubting believer to climb over, but rather as an open-armed welcome of assurance and comfort.

If I may illustrate. When hill-walking, I have from time to time missed my path and come up against a stone wall topped by barbed wire. Yet, if I had taken the right path, I would have met another wall straddled by a ladder stile. John did not write his book to confront his readers with a stone wall topped by barbed wire! He wrote to enable his readers to get over their fears: 'I write these things to you who believe in the name of the Son of God *so that you may know* that you have eternal life' (1 John 5:13). The same may be said about his remarks as he drew near the close of his Gospel, when John explained why he had written that volume: 'That you may believe that Jesus is the Christ, the Son of God, and that by believing you may have life in his name' (John 20:31). Remember that in both works he was writing to believers. He wanted unbelievers to hear the truth, believe and be converted, yes, but he also wanted (perhaps, primarily he wanted) believers to read and go on believing – being confirmed in their faith.

If I may be permitted a further illustration. The bread knife! An excellent tool, one well designed for the job – cutting bread. It has a comfortable handle and a sharp blade. Catch hold of the knife by the handle, and it can be used to slice crusty bread with ease. Catch hold of it by the blade, however, and while the handle will make little impression on the bread, the blade will make a nasty impression on the palm of your hand.

I am reminded of the way hyper-Calvinists read the invitations of the gospel. Take Matthew 11:28, for instance: 'Come to me, all you who are weary and burdened, and I will give you rest'. So said Christ. Now, how should we take hold of this invitation? Should we pore over our hearts to see if we are weary, if we are weary enough, before we feel that we are invited to come to Christ? Or should we take the invitation – as Jesus clearly intended we should – and treat his words as the warmest, widest and freest of invitations? Surely, Jesus was not making sinners think about themselves, but encouraging them to think of him, and, above all urging them to come to himself for salvation and rest!

Thus it is with John's tests. While they *can* be misread as introspective hindrances to the doubting soul, they are clearly meant as the warmest of encouragements, designed by the apostle to put doubting souls at rest.

I go further. There is no man alive – John, himself, certainly was no exception – there is no man alive who can honestly say he fulfils any of these tests as well as he should. Not one! But John was not demanding perfection! If perfection is required before we can be assured, then there's not a true believer on the face of the globe! Having said that, yet again I have to sound the note on the other string: not demanding perfection is not the same as *laissez-faire*. The truth is, the question is: Do I have a desire to meet John's tests? Do I, for example, desire to love and obey Christ? Do I want to love my brothers? Do I have any measure of love towards Christ? Can I detect any mark of obedience to Christ? Do I want to obey Christ?

As William Cowper has it:

> *Lord, it is my chief complaint*
> *That my love is weak and faint;*
> *Yet I love thee, and adore:*
> *O for grace to love thee more!*

In other words, we must not raise the barrier so high that nobody can get over. Rather, we must follow the apostle, and bring it as low as John himself did, in order that all believers might receive all the assurance he desired for them. As Calvin commented on 1 John 2:3: 'We know that we have come to know him if we obey his commands':

We are not hence to conclude that faith recumbs [leans, rests, reposes] on works: for though every one receives a testimony to his faith from his works, yet it does not follow that it is founded on them, since they are added as an evidence... The certainty of faith depends on the grace of Christ alone, but piety and holiness of life distinguish true faith from the knowledge of God which is fictitious and dead (Col. 3:9).

Again, Calvin on 1 John 3:14: 'We know that we have passed from death to life, because we love our brothers':

Were it said that love makes us more certain of life, then confidence as to salvation would recumb [lean, rest, repose] on works. But the answer to this is obvious: for though faith is confirmed by all the graces of God as aids, yet it ceases not to have its foundation in the mercy of God only.

Again, Calvin on 1 John 3:18-20: 'Dear children, let us not love with words or tongue but with actions and in truth. This then is how we know that we belong to the truth, and how we set our hearts at rest in his presence whenever our hearts condemn us':

If we, in truth, love our neighbours, we have an evidence that we are born of God, who is truth, or that the truth of God dwells in us. But we must ever remember that we have not from love the knowledge which the apostle mentions, as though we were to seek from it the certainty of salvation. And doubtless we know not otherwise that we are the children of God, than as he seals his free adoption on our hearts by his own Spirit, and as we receive by faith the sure pledge of it offered in Christ. Then love is accessory or an inferior aid, a prop to our faith, not a foundation on which it rests. Why then does the apostle say: 'We shall assure our hearts before God'? He reminds us by these words that faith does not exist without a good conscience; not that assurance arises from it or depends on it, but that then only we are really and not falsely assured of our union with God, when by the efficacy of his Holy Spirit he manifests himself in our love. For it is ever meet and proper to consider what the apostle handles. For as he condemns feigned and false profession of faith, he says that a genuine assurance before God we cannot have, except his Spirit produces in us the fruit of love. Nevertheless, though a good conscience cannot be separated from faith, yet no one should hence conclude that we must look to our works in order that our assurance may be certain.

Finally, Calvin on 1 John 5:13-14: 'I write these things to you who believe in the name of the Son of God so that you may know that you have eternal life. This is the confidence we have in approaching God: that if we ask anything according to his will, he hears us':

As there ought to be a daily progress in faith, so [John] says that he wrote to those who had already believed, so that they might believe more firmly and with greater certainty, and thus enjoy a fuller confidence as to eternal life. Then the use of doctrine is not only to initiate the ignorant in the knowledge of Christ, but also to confirm those more and more who have been already taught. It therefore becomes us assiduously to attend to the duty of learning, that our faith may increase through the whole course of our life. For there are still in us many remnants of unbelief, and so weak is our faith that what we believe is not yet really believed except there be a fuller confirmation.

And now a most important statement:

But we ought to observe the way in which faith is confirmed, even by having the office and power of Christ explained to us. For the apostle says that he wrote these things, that is, that eternal life is to be sought nowhere else but in Christ, in order that they who were believers already might believe, that is, make progress in believing. It is therefore the duty of a godly teacher, in order to confirm disciples in the faith, to extol as much as possible the grace of Christ, so that being satisfied with that, we may seek nothing else.

Those words must sink in! Calvin went on:

The apostle teaches further still... that Christ is the peculiar object of faith, and that to the faith which we have in his name is annexed the hope of salvation. For in this case the end of believing is that we become the children and the heirs of God.

As for : 'And this is the confidence', Calvin declared:

[John] commends the faith which he mentioned by its fruit, or he shows that in which our confidence especially is, that is, that the godly dare confidently to call on God; as also Paul speaks in Ephesians 3:12, that we have by faith access to God with confidence; and also in

Romans 8:15, that the Spirit gives us a mouth to cry: 'Abba, Father'. And doubtless, were we driven away from an access to God, nothing could make us more miserable; but, on the other hand, provided this asylum [refuge] be opened to us, we should be happy even in extreme evils; indeed, this one thing renders our troubles blessed, because we surely know that God will be our deliverer, and relying on his paternal love towards us, we flee to him. Let us, then, bear in mind this declaration of the apostle, that calling on God is the chief trial of our faith, and that God is not rightly nor in faith called upon except we be fully persuaded that our prayers will not be in vain. For the apostle denies that those who, being doubtful, hesitate, are endued with faith.[9]

And now Spurgeon – on 1 John 5:13:

John then proceeds to mention three witnesses. Now, dear hearers, do you know anything about these three witnesses?... Do you know 'the Spirit'? Has the Spirit of God quickened you, changed you, illuminated you, sanctified you? Does the Spirit of God dwell in you? Do you feel his sacred impulses? Is he the essence of the new life within you? Do you know him as clothing you with his light and power? If so, you are alive unto God... One thing more I would notice. Read the ninth verse: the apostle puts our faith and assurance on the ground that we receive 'the witness of God'. If I believe that I am saved because of this, that, and the other, I may be mistaken: the only sure ground is 'the witness of God'. The inmost heart of Christian faith is that we take God at his word; and we must accept that word, not because of the probabilities of its statements, nor because of the confirmatory evidence of science and philosophy, but simply and alone because the Lord has spoken it. Many professing Christians fall sadly short of this point. They dare to judge the word instead of bowing before it. They do not sit at the Master's feet, but become doctors themselves. I thank God that I believe everything that God has spoken, whether I am able to see its reason or not. To me the fact that the mouth of God hath spoken it stands in the place of all argument, either for or against. If Jehovah says so, so it is. Do you accept the witness of God? If not, you have made him a liar, and the truth is not in you; but if you have received 'the witness of God', then this is his witness, that 'he has given to us eternal life, and this life is in his Son'. I say again, if your faith stands in the wisdom of men, and is based upon the cleverness of a preacher, it will fail you; but if it stands on the sure word of the Lord it will stand for ever, and this may be to you a special token that you have eternal life. I have said enough upon this subject; oh that God may bless it to

[9] Here, once again, is Calvin's view that assurance is the essence of faith.

you! May we be enabled, from what John has written, to gather beyond doubt that we have the life of God within our souls... John desired the increase and confirmation of their faith. He says: 'That you might believe on the name of the Son of God'. John wrote to those who believed, that they might believe in a more emphatic sense. As our Saviour has come not only that we may have life, but that we may have it more abundantly, so does John write, that having faith we may have more of it. Come, beloved, listen for a moment to this! You have the milk of faith, but God wills that you should have this cream of assurance! He would increase your faith...

Will you live in perpetual questioning and doubt?... The Bible is sent that you may have full assurance of your possession of eternal life; do not, therefore, dream that it will be presumptuous on your part to aspire to it. Our conscience tells us that we ought to seek full assurance of salvation. It cannot be right for us to be children of God, and not to know our own Father. How can we kneel down and say: 'Our Father which art in heaven', when we do not know whether he is our Father or not? Will not a life of doubt tend to be a life of falsehood? May we not be using language which is not true to our consciousness? Can you sing joyful hymns which you fear are not true to you? Will you join in worship when your heart does not know that God is your God? Until the spirit of adoption enables you to cry, 'Abba, Father', where is your love to God? Can you rest? Dare you rest, while it is a question whether you are saved or not? Can you go home to your dinner today and enjoy your meal, while there is a question about your soul's eternal life? Oh, be not so foolhardy as to run risks on that matter! I pray you, make sure work for eternity. If you leave anything in uncertainty, let it concern your body or your estate, but not your soul. Conscience bids you seek to know that you have eternal life, for without this knowledge many duties will be impossible of performance. Many scriptures which I cannot quote this morning stir you up to this duty. Are you not bidden to make your calling and election sure? Are you not a thousand times over exhorted to rejoice in the Lord, and to give thanks continually? But how can you rejoice, if the dark suspicion haunts you, that perhaps, after all, you have not the life of God? You must get this question settled, or you cannot rest in the Lord, and wait patiently for him. Come, brothers and sisters, I beseech you, as you would follow Scripture, and obey the Lord's precepts, get the assurance without which you cannot obey them.

Listen, as I close, to this mass of reasons why each believer should seek to know that he has eternal life. Here they are. Assurance of your salvation will bring you 'the peace of God, which passes all understanding'... Assurance is a mountain of spices, a land that flows with milk and honey. To be the assured possessor of eternal life is to find a paradise beneath the stars, where the mountains and the hills break forth before you into singing.

Full assurance will sometimes overflow in cataracts of delight. Peace flows like a river, and here and there it leaps in cascades of ecstatic joy. There are seasons when the plant of peace is in flower, and then it sheds a perfume as of myrrh and cassia. Oh, the blessedness of the man who knows that he has eternal life! Sometimes in our room alone, when we have been enjoying this assurance, we have laughed outright, for we could not help it. If anybody had wondered why a man was laughing by himself alone, we could have explained that it was nothing ridiculous which had touched us, but our mouth was filled with laughter because the Lord had done great things for us, whereof we were glad. That religion which sets no sweetmeats on the table is a niggardly housekeeper. I do not wonder that some people give up their starveling religion: it is hardly worth the keeping. The child of God who knows that he has eternal life goes to school, but he has many a holiday; and he anticipates that day of home-going when he shall see the face of his beloved for ever.

Brethren, full assurance will give us the full result of the gospel. The gospel ought to make us holy; and so it will when we are in full possession of it. The gospel ought to make us separate from the world, the gospel ought to make us lead a heavenly life here below; and so it will if we drink deep draughts of it; but it we take only a sip of it now and again, we give it no chance of working out its design in us. Do not paddle about the margin of the water of life, but first wade in up to your knees, and then hasten to plunge into the waters to swim in. Beware of contentment with shallow grace. Prove what the grace of God can do for you by giving yourself up to its power.

Full assurance gives a man a grateful zeal for the God he loves.[10] These are the people that will go to the Congo for Jesus, for they know they are his. These are the people that will lay down their all for Christ, for Christ is theirs. These are the people that will bear scorn and shame and misrepresentation for the truth's sake, for they know that they have eternal life. These are they that will keep on preaching and teaching, spending and working, for theirs is the kingdom of heaven, and they know it. Men will do little for what they doubt, and much for what they believe. If you have lost your title deeds, and you do not know whether your house is your own or not, you are not going to spend much in repairs and enlargements. When you know that heaven is yours, you

---

[10] 'Assurance of salvation is one of the greatest motivators in the New Testament' (Eaton: *1,2,3 John* p63).

are anxious to get ready for it. Full assurance finds fuel for zeal to feed upon.

This also creates and sustains patience. When we know that we have eternal life, we do not fret about the trials of this passing life... Assurance makes us strong to suffer.

This, dear friends, will give you constant firmness in your confession of divine truth. You who do not know whether you are saved or not, I hope the Lord will keep you from denying the faith; but those who have a firm grip of it, these are the men who will never forsake it... When you know that your Lord is able to keep that which you have committed to him until that day, then you are firm as a rock. God make you so.

Dear brethren, this is the kind of thing that will enable you to bear a telling testimony for your Lord. It is of no use to stand up and preach things that may or may not be true. I am charged with being a dreadful dogmatist, and I am not anxious to excuse myself. When a man is not quite sure of a thing, he grows very liberal [unstable, undogmatic, erratic, wavering]...

God grant that you may have this assurance, all of you! May sinners begin to believe in Jesus, and saints believe more firmly, for Christ's sake! Amen.[11]

Out of the wealth of gems in the above, because it captures precisely what John's first letter is about, I select this: 'John desired the increase and confirmation of their faith'. He was not setting out a series of hurdles over which his readers had to jump in order to get assurance.

Let me apply this to those of us who preach in a stated way. If ever there was a time when we need to openly and clearly distinguish in our ministry between the unbeliever and the believer, this is it. Indeed, on this issue we need to distinguish between the unbeliever, 'the carnal Christian' (so-called), the false professor, the doubting believer, and the assured believer. What we must not do is grab a text and go at it like a bull in the proverbial china shop! If we do, we risk making true believers wrongly unhappy – that is, quench the smoking flax. Of course, if we at the same time alarm the careless and sanctify the carnal, that may be considered a price worth paying. I don't! There's no need of it! With due care, it is

---

[11] Sermon number 2023. See also sermon number 1791.

surely possible to meet all those proper ends, and yet *not* break any bruised reeds on the way.

In the body of the book, I quoted John Macarthur. I do so again as a warning to us all. Macarthur was not sufficiently nuanced here, and I can only guess as to the hurt his words may have caused:

I think it's fair to say the pulpit is *rightly* the creator of anxious hearts. That's part of the duty of the preacher – to make the heart anxious... The pulpit is to be a purveyor of a message that creates anxious hearts... Where there is that strong preaching, there will be a battle with assurance. And I'll tell you something, it's not bad to have that; it's good because how else are we drawn to the important issue of self-examination?[12]

I am sure that the words of John – John, the apostle – properly interpreted, will reassure the doubting believer, while at the same time they rightly disabuse the unbeliever.

---

[12] 'Why Christians Lack Assurance', emphasis mine.

Appendix 4

2 Corinthians 13:5

On my return I will not spare those who sinned earlier or any of the others, since you are demanding proof that Christ is speaking through me. He is not weak in dealing with you, but is powerful among you. For to be sure, he was crucified in weakness, yet he lives by God's power. Likewise, we are weak in him, yet by God's power we will live with him to serve you. Examine yourselves to see whether you are in the faith; test yourselves. Do you not realise that Christ Jesus is in you – unless, of course, you fail the test? And I trust that you will discover that we have not failed the test. Now we pray to God that you will not do anything wrong. Not that people will see that we have stood the test but that you will do what is right even though we may seem to have failed (2 Cor. 13:2-7).

The relevant portion is, of course: 'Examine yourselves to see whether you are in the faith; test yourselves'. But, as always, the context is vital, and that is why I have supplied it.

When Paul told the Corinthians: 'Examine yourselves to see whether you are in the faith; test yourselves', he was not calling them to harrowing self-doubt about the reality of their faith. This is usually assumed, but it's quite foreign to the passage.

For a start, Paul was not addressing the believers at Corinth as individuals. The context tells us that the apostle was under attack over his apostleship and his ministry; and by the context I mean not only the immediate verses, but the entire letter. The Judaisers were infiltrating and subverting the church at Corinth. And they were putting Paul and his ministry under the microscope, using the Corinthians as a cat's-paw. Paul responded. Having fought it out with the Judaisers in the earlier part of his letter (from 2 Cor. 2:14 and on) – just as he did with the Judaisers at Philippi (Phil. 3:2-11, and on) – as he comes to the end of his letter, the apostle swings the spotlight onto the Corinthians. Not that he was paying them back in kind, giving them as good as he got! Paul was no small-minded bigot! No! He was fighting (spiritually) tooth and nail for the gospel against the law mongers: 'You took the side of the Judaisers, and tested me', he thundered. 'Right! Now take your own medicine.

Take your diaries out and jog your memory as to how you got where you are!' Just as he addressed them in 2 Corinthians 3, so he does here. Let me remind you of what he said in the earlier passage:

Thanks be to God, who always leads us in triumphal procession in Christ and through us spreads everywhere the fragrance of the knowledge of him. For we are to God the aroma of Christ among those who are being saved and those who are perishing. To the one we are the smell of death; to the other, the fragrance of life. And who is equal to such a task? Unlike so many, we do not peddle the word of God for profit. On the contrary, in Christ we speak before God with sincerity, like men sent from God. Are we beginning to commend ourselves again? Or do we need, like some people, letters of recommendation to you or from you? You yourselves are our letter, written on our hearts, known and read by everybody. You show that you are a letter from Christ, the result of our ministry, written not with ink but with the Spirit of the living God, not on tablets of stone but on tablets of human hearts. Such confidence as this is ours through Christ before God. Not that we are competent in ourselves to claim anything for ourselves, but our competence comes from God. He has made us competent as ministers of a new covenant – not of the letter but of the Spirit; for the letter kills, but the Spirit gives life (2 Cor. 2:14 – 3:6).

And now the present passage:

On my return I will not spare those who sinned earlier or any of the others, since you are demanding proof that Christ is speaking through me. He is not weak in dealing with you, but is powerful among you. For to be sure, he was crucified in weakness, yet he lives by God's power. Likewise, we are weak in him, yet by God's power we will live with him to serve you. Examine yourselves to see whether you are in the faith; test yourselves. Do you not realise that Christ Jesus is in you – unless, of course, you fail the test? And I trust that you will discover that we have not failed the test (2 Cor. 13:2-6).

The apostle's meaning is patent. Addressing the believers at Corinth as a whole – not the individual believer – addressing the Corinthian church as a church, and calling on the church to speak up, in effect he was saying: 'Take a good look at your experience! I am talking to you Corinthians as a body! Did you at Corinth receive Christ through the Judaisers and their law preaching? Of course you didn't! It was through my ministry that you heard of Christ, it was though my new-covenant ministry that you came to Christ, and thus received all the benefits stored up in Christ! Speak up! Own it for the truth that it is! Unless, of course, you are reprobates!' As he reminded them, clearly with the Judaisers in mind, and with irony: 'Even though you have ten thousand guardians in Christ, you do not have many fathers, for in Christ Jesus I became your father through the gospel' (1 Cor. 4:15).

I think we ought to refresh our memory of all that had gone on at Corinth. Here's Luke's record of those events:

Paul left Athens and went to Corinth. There he met a Jew named Aquila, a native of Pontus, who had recently come from Italy with his wife Priscilla, because Claudius had ordered all the Jews to leave Rome. Paul went to see them, and because he was a tentmaker as they were, he stayed and worked with them. Every Sabbath he reasoned in the synagogue, trying to persuade Jews and Greeks. When Silas and Timothy came from Macedonia, Paul devoted himself exclusively to preaching, testifying to the Jews that Jesus was the Christ. But when the Jews opposed Paul and became abusive, he shook out his clothes in protest and said to them: 'Your blood be on your own heads! I am clear of my responsibility. From now on I will go to the Gentiles'. Then Paul left the synagogue and went next door to the house of Titius Justus, a worshipper of God. Crispus, the synagogue ruler, and his entire household believed in the Lord; and many of the Corinthians who heard him believed and were baptised. One night the Lord spoke to Paul in a vision: 'Do not be afraid; keep on speaking, do not be silent. For I am with you, and no one is going to attack and harm you, because I have many people in this city'. So Paul stayed for a year and a half, teaching them the word of God (Acts 18:1-11).

And we know what Paul preached – and it wasn't law. As he told the Corinthians:

We preach Christ crucified... I resolved to know nothing while I was with you except Jesus Christ and him crucified... Woe to me if I do not preach the gospel!... Now, brothers, I want to remind you of the gospel I preached to you, which you received and on which you have taken your stand. By this gospel you are saved, if you hold firmly to the word I preached to you. Otherwise, you have believed in vain. For what I received I passed on to you as of first importance: that Christ died for our sins according to the Scriptures, that he was buried, that he was raised on the third day according to the Scriptures... This is what we preach, and this is what you believed (1 Cor. 2:2; 1:23; 9:16; 15:1-11).

Now if the ministry that brought death, which was engraved in letters on stone, came with glory, so that the Israelites could not look steadily at the face of Moses because of its glory, fading though it was, will not the ministry of the Spirit be even more glorious? If the ministry that condemns men is glorious, how much more glorious is the ministry that brings righteousness! For what was glorious has no glory now in comparison with the surpassing glory. And if what was fading away came with glory, how much greater is the glory of that which lasts! Therefore, since we have such a hope, we are very bold... Now the Lord is the Spirit, and where the Spirit of the Lord is, there is freedom. And we, who with unveiled faces all reflect the Lord's glory, are being transformed into his likeness with ever-increasing glory, which comes from the Lord, who is the Spirit. Therefore, since through God's mercy we have this ministry, we do not lose heart. Rather, we have renounced secret and shameful ways; we do not use deception, nor do we distort the word of God. On the contrary, by setting forth the truth plainly we commend ourselves to every man's conscience in the sight of God... We do not preach ourselves, but Jesus Christ as Lord, and ourselves as your servants for Jesus' sake. For God... made his light shine in our hearts to give us the light of the knowledge of the glory of God in the face of Christ (2 Cor. 3:7 – 4:6).

In short, Paul is not calling the Corinthians to rake over their souls to see if they were genuine believers. Rather, because they were genuine believers, he is calling on them to ask themselves how they became such. Was it by the law preachers, or by his ministry of the gospel in the power and demonstration of the Spirit? Did he not preach Christ – not law – and was it not Christ who brought them to where they are now? Not only must the Corinthians not forget their history, they must speak up, throw over the Judaisers and their law teaching, and stand with the apostle for Christ and under Christ!

Do not miss the apostle's use of irony – not to say sarcasm – in all this: 'I trust you will find that you are real Christians! I trust you will find I am!' And this takes me to what might be considered the clinching point in this exegesis. If the 'usual' view is right, and Paul is commanding believers – in the first instance, the Corinthians – to probe themselves to try to get assurance, then we end up with the distinct possibility that his first readers might do as he commands, and not only test themselves, but put the apostle himself and Timothy through it! And they should do this to see whether or not the pair were true believers! What is more, he hopes that they will find that he and Timothy do indeed have enough evidence to pass muster! Worse – even if the Corinthians discover that he and Timothy are *not* true believers, he hopes that the Corinthians themselves will still go on to the end! An exegesis conceived in cloud cuckoo land, surely!

The notion that Paul here drives every individual believer into self-doubt is far removed from this passage. The context is entirely corporate – not the individual believer, but the whole church at Corinth. And that church must own up and confess that it was Paul's ministry of Christ and his gospel, and not the Judaisers with their law mongering, that had brought them into blessing. 'Examine yourselves', Paul demanded. 'You received Christ through my ministry, didn't you!'

Of course, I am not saying that the passage has nothing to say to us today, and say to us individually – both believer and unbeliever – but we must not miss the main thrust of the apostle's words. What is more, 2 Corinthians could hardly be more relevant, faced as we are with so many law preachers. Contemporary law preachers have a great deal more in common with the Judaisers than they like to recognise.

This is not the only place where we find the apostle taking such a tack. Listen to the parallel in the opening of Galatians 3:

You foolish Galatians! Who has bewitched you? Before your very eyes Jesus Christ was clearly portrayed as crucified. I would like to learn just one thing from you: Did you receive the Spirit by observing the law, or by believing what you heard? Are you so foolish? After beginning with the Spirit, are you now trying to attain your goal by human effort? Have you suffered so much for nothing – if it really was for nothing? Does God give you his Spirit and work miracles among you because you observe the law, or because you believe what you heard? (Gal. 3:1-5).

The Galatians – as so many churches in the New Testament – were also being attacked by the Judaisers with their law mongering, and Paul stood up to them through the Galatians. Note the same irony here, as in the Corinthian letter, the same demand for a 100% endorsement of the apostle's work in the ministry of the new covenant by the Spirit, and not by the law. As he went on to say to the Galatians:

Formerly, when you did not know God, you were slaves to those who by nature are not gods. But now that you know God – or rather are known by God – how is it that you are turning back to those weak and miserable principles? Do you wish to be enslaved by them all over again? You are observing special days and months and seasons and years! I fear for you, that somehow I have wasted my efforts on you. I plead with you, brothers, become like me, for I became like you. You have done me no wrong. As you know, it was because of an illness that I first preached the gospel to you. Even though my illness was a trial to you, you did not treat me with contempt or scorn. Instead, you welcomed me as if I were an angel of God, as if I were Christ Jesus himself. What has happened to all your joy? I can testify that, if you could have done so, you would have torn out your eyes and given them to me. Have I now become your enemy by telling you the truth? Those people are zealous to win you over, but for no good. What they want is to alienate you [from us], so that you may be zealous for them. It is fine to be zealous, provided the purpose is good, and to be so always and not just when I am with you. My dear children, for whom I am again in the pains of childbirth until Christ is formed in you, how I wish I could be with you now and change my tone, because I am perplexed about you! (Gal. 4:8-20).

In short, 2 Corinthians 13:5 is not a call for every individual believer to put himself on the rack to try to find if he is a true believer. Rather, it is a demand for endorsement – by the Corinthians – of the apostle's ministry of the Spirit as opposed to the ministry of law.

J.N.Darby:

[The apostle]... puts an end to the question about his ministry by presenting an idea which ought to confound them utterly. If Christ had not spoken by him, Christ did not dwell in them. If Christ was in them, he must have spoken by the apostle, for he had been the means of their conversion. 'Since', he says, 'you seek a proof that Christ speaks in me, examine yourselves, whether you are in the faith. Do you not know yourselves, that Christ dwells in you, unless you are reprobates?' And that they did not at all think. This was quite upsetting to them, and turning their foolish and stupid opposition, their unbecoming contempt for the apostle, to their own confusion. What folly to allow themselves to be led away by a thought which, no doubt, exalted them in their own eyes, but which, by calling in question the apostleship of Paul, necessarily overturned, at the same time, their own experience [Darby had 'Christianity']![1]

As Calvin observed,[2] Paul was appealing to the church – challenging the church – to admit that everything they had received by way of spiritual benefit in Christ, they had received through his ministry. That was the thrust of his demand to examine themselves. The apostle was not telling them to probe themselves as to the reality of their faith.

Calvin:

[Paul] confirms, what he had stated previously – that Christ's power showed itself openly in his ministry. For he makes them [the Corinthians] the judges of this matter, provided they descend, as it were, into themselves, and acknowledge what they had received from him. In the first place, as there is but one Christ, it must be of necessity, that the same Christ must dwell alike in minister and people. Now, dwelling in the people, how will he deny himself in the minister? Further, he had shown his power in Paul's preaching, in such a manner that it could be no longer doubtful or obscure to the Corinthians, if they were not altogether stupid. For, whence had they faith? Whence had they Christ? Whence, *in fine*, had they everything? It is with good reason, therefore, that they are called to look into themselves, that they may discover there, what they despise as a thing unknown. Then only has a minister a true and well grounded assurance for the approbation of his doctrine, when he can appeal to the consciences of those whom he has taught, that, if they have anything of Christ, and of sincere piety, they may be constrained to acknowledge his fidelity. We are now in possession of Paul's object.

Calvin went on to argue against 'the Sorbonnic sophists' (Roman schoolmen) – who denied the possibility of assurance, leaving us believers – 'our consciences' – 'constantly in suspense, and in a state of perplexity'. Calvin immediately went on:

But what does Paul say here? He declares that all are reprobates, who doubt whether they profess Christ and are a part of his body. Let us, therefore, reckon that alone to be right [true, saving] faith, which leads us to repose in safety in the favour of God, with no wavering opinion, but with a firm and steadfast assurance.

---

[1] Darby pp387-388.

[2] In his *Commentaries*.

Calvin saw that Paul, in 2 Corinthians 13, was not setting out to make believers anxious, but, taking their conversion as a reality, he was using that fact to vindicate his ministry of Christ by the Spirit in the face of the Judaisers and their emphasis upon law.

When Calvin said: 'Paul... declares that all are reprobates, who doubt whether they profess Christ and are a part of his body', he went too far. It is possible for believers to have doubt, and yet still be true believers – as I have shown from 1 John.[3] Nevertheless, every believer ought to enjoy the fullest possible sense of assurance. Paul was able to appeal to it in his battle with the Judaisers. And assurance should be the norm today. It was in the New Testament. And it should be for us. That is why I have written this book. Law teachers bring believers into serious bondage. They preach and teach in such a way as to produce anxiety in believers. Amazing! Are these men gospel preachers or law preachers? 2 Corinthians 13:5 stands as a mighty challenge to all believers: Do you want law or grace?

---

[3] See the previous Appendix.

Appendix 5
1 Corinthians 11:28

Whoever eats the bread or drinks the cup of the Lord in an unworthy manner will be guilty of sinning against the body and blood of the Lord. A man ought to examine himself before he eats of the bread and drinks of the cup. For anyone who eats and drinks without recognising the body of the Lord eats and drinks judgement on himself. That is why many among you are weak and sick, and a number of you have fallen asleep. But if we judged ourselves, we would not come under judgement (1 Cor. 11:27-31).

The relevant extract is, of course: 'A man ought to examine himself'; that is, a believer ought to examine himself. But, since it is vital, I have quoted the context. The context, as always, is king!

And what does that context tells us? The passage is entirely concerned, solely concerned, with a believer preparing himself for the Lord's supper. It has nothing to do with making a Christian doubt his salvation, urging a believer to test himself as to the reality of his faith; *that* is utterly foreign to the context. In other words, the passage does not in any way support the view that believers must look to their sanctification for assurance. The apostle's words are, from first to last, to do with the believer in his approach to the breaking of bread in remembrance of Christ, his Lord and Saviour.

By plucking the command out of context, by ignoring the context, of course, a legal preacher can have a field-day. He can misuse the passage to make a believer doubt whether or not he is in the faith. He can point to the gloomy portals of introspection, and bid the believer enter! Moreover, the individual believer can take the text, and do all this for himself. Thus by grabbing this command out of context, the believer can be driven – or drive himself – into a whirlpool of sadness and doubt. And I am sure the devil will not be slow in making him do it! And all the time, as I say, the apostle's command is to do with preparation for the Lord's supper.

Nor should we miss, even in the call for self-examination before taking the supper, the apostle's positive and encouraging tone, as it is brought out in the NKJV: 'But let a man examine himself, *and so let him eat of the bread and drink of the cup'*. Yet again, we see that the notion that Paul was driving believers into introspection, making them anxious, is a million miles away from the context.

Calvin, commenting on the passage, rightly dismissed the papist nonsense of 'auricular confession', calling it 'torture': 'Those persons, after having tortured themselves with reflection for a few hours, and making the priest – such as he is – privy to their vileness, imagine that they have done their duty. It is an examination of another sort that Paul here requires'. And, of course, something similar (leaving aside the aspect of confession to a priest) could be said about any form of legal teaching which encourages doubt and introspection.

Paul's purpose – 'an examination of another sort that Paul here requires' – is all to do with the Lord's supper. Calvin again:

If you would wish to use aright the benefit afforded by Christ, bring faith and repentance. As to these two things, therefore, the trial must be made, if you would come duly prepared. Under repentance I include love; for the man who has learned to renounce himself, that he may give himself up wholly to Christ and his service, will also, without doubt, carefully maintain that unity which Christ has enjoined.

And even in saying this, being sensitive to the fears of believers, Calvin went on: 'It is not a perfect faith or repentance that is required, as some, by urging beyond due bounds, a perfection that can nowhere be found, would shut out for ever from the supper every individual of mankind'. The upshot? 'If, however, you aspire after the righteousness of God with the earnest desire of your mind, and, trembling under a view of your misery, do wholly lean upon Christ's grace', come to the table. In other words, the believer must examine himself, but even in this he must not expect perfection before he can go to the supper. 'Do you want to wholly lean on Christ and his grace?' Then come! I say again, the apostle does not command the believer to search himself as to whether or not he is a believer!

Good as his comments are, nevertheless Calvin did not get to the heart of what Paul was saying, but he did come close with his: 'Carefully maintain that unity which Christ has enjoined'. Let me explain. Let us think a little more about 'recognising the body' of Christ. This is generally assumed, I think, to be 'recognising the body of Christ, Christ's own body, pictured in the elements'. This may be right. Even so, almost certainly, the apostle includes – if he does not concentrate on – the body of Christ in the sense of 'the church'.

Fee:

> The bread does refer to Christ's physical body that was given in death on the cross. But the meaning of that 'body' at this table is that those who eat the one loaf are themselves that one body... The Lord's supper is not just any meal; it is *the* meal, in which at a common table, with one loaf and a common cup they proclaimed that through the death of Christ they were one body, the body of Christ; and therefore they are not just any group of sociologically diverse people who could keep those differences intact at this table. Here they must 'discern/recognise as distinct' the one body of Christ, of which they are all parts and in which they are all gifts to one another. To fail to discern the body in this way, by abusing those of lesser sociological status, is to incur God's judgement.[1]

This is right. Take Paul's earlier words:

> Is not the cup of thanksgiving for which we give thanks a participation in the blood of Christ? And is not the bread that we break a participation in the body of Christ? Because there is one loaf, we, who are many, are one body, for we all partake of the one loaf (1 Cor. 10:16-17; see also 1 Cor. 12:12-27).[2]

As a result, I do not discount 'regard for the body of Christ pictured in the elements', but I am sure that 'regard for, love for, the members of Christ with whom I am about the break bread' also figures prominently in 'recognising the Lord's body', especially bearing in mind how necessary this rebuke was at Corinth. At the supper itself, the believers were appallingly carnal in their division and disregard for each other (1 Cor. 11:17-21), and God had judged them with sickness and death because of it (1 Cor. 11:29-30). And it was not just at the supper. The church was riddled with division, party spirit, cliques, carnality, toleration of dreadful offences, going

---

[1] Fee: *1 Corinthians* p564, emphasis his. Fee cited Isa. 1:14-17.

[2] Calvin commented: 'The Corinthians [must] understand that we must, even by external profession, maintain that unity which subsists between us and Christ, inasmuch as we all assemble together to receive the symbol of that sacred unity'.

to law with each other, proud excesses in their assemblies, and so on. I can quite see why Paul tackled this by urging his readers to 'discern the Lord's body'.

In any case, whichever of the two meanings we attach to 'the body' – or both – *the apostle is not calling the Corinthians to harrowing self-doubt as to the reality of their faith.* Rather, he demands that the believer searches himself as to his love for Christ expressed in his love for fellow-believers – the very ones with whom he is about to break bread. This is all of a piece with Christ's words (rightly understanding his allusion to 'altar', of course):

Therefore, if you are offering your gift at the altar and there remember that your brother has something against you, leave your gift there in front of the altar. First go and be reconciled to your brother; then come and offer your gift (Matt. 5:23-24).

None of this is designed to make a believer doubt the reality of his experience.

Spurgeon spoke of the process known as 'fencing the table'. He explained this 'fencing'. It is, he said, 'defending the table of the Lord against the approach of improper characters'. Acknowledging the rightness of the practice, even so he was clear that some had gone too far with it, and caused much hurt thereby:

This [fencing] is a very right and necessary thing to do, but some ministers have so guarded the table that very few have dared to come to it – and those who have come have often been persons who had more conceit than grace, while the better part – the truly humble and broken-hearted ones – have been frightened away! It would appear, from the exhortations of these ministers, as if Paul must have said: 'Let a man examine himself, but never let him eat of this bread, nor drink of this cup. Let him so examine himself that he shall come to the conclusion that he has no right to sit at the table of the Lord and, therefore, shall go his way feeling that he is utterly unworthy of that high privilege'. Beloved friends, this is not my objective in preaching from this text, nor should it be yours in obeying it. Examine yourselves with the hope and the strong desire that you may be permitted to come to the Lord's table. Do not let the examination take so morbid and melancholy a form that you almost look out for causes of self-suspicion, but the rather, especially as many of you have known the Lord for years, let your examination be made in order that you may come aright to the table, that you may come there in a right spirit, and not that you may be compelled to stay away. 'Let a man examine himself', and then, in the spirit of self-examination, let him eat of this bread, and drink of this cup.

Spurgeon went on to reassure believers:

Distinctly remember that the qualification for a place at the Lord's table is *not* perfect sanctification. If it were, I am afraid that there would not be a soul here so qualified. And if there should be one who declared that he had attained to such a state, I should expect that he would prove to be the biggest hypocrite in the place! Recollect, also, that the qualification for coming to the Lord's table is not the full assurance of faith. There might be some genuine believers in Christ who would not be able to commune if that were the qualification, but, happily, it is not. The least grain of true faith in Christ qualifies you! You are not to examine to see whether it is full noontide with your soul – have you even a little twilight? Have you been quickened into new life so much as to have a holy hunger and thirst for more of the Christ who is already yours? If so, you may come to his table. Do not arrange the examination in such a way as to exclude yourselves unnecessarily. I will not, if I can help it, put it in such a style as to exclude one of you who ought to be admitted. On the contrary, my soul longs that the whole of you might truly feel and say: 'Yes, we do love the Lord, and we are anxious to come and obey his command, and thus show his death in remembrance of him'. Well, that is the first great objective of this examination – not that you may be made to stay away, but that you may come, if you are really entitled to sit at the table of your Lord!

Let me continue with Spurgeon – even though he has said enough on this head to make the point. Note his warm and encouraging words from this passage, words to encourage doubting believers to come to assurance:

And, surely, it also means that every communicant must come most humbly, for the result of any true examination of ourselves must be deep humiliation of spirit. As for myself, I must confess that I am not what I want to be, and I am not what I ought to be. I can only come to the table declaring myself to be an unworthy one in whom the grace of God is indeed magnified. That he should ever have put me among his children and permitted me to call him, my Father, will be a wonder to me throughout eternity! See, then, the blessed result of this self-examination when it lays you low at the foot of the cross, and makes you come to the Lord's table, not boasting: 'I have a right to be here', but humbly and gratefully saying: 'I do indeed adore the grace of God which has made it possible that such an one as I am should be allowed to sit down with the family of God at his banqueting table of love'.

And yet more:

And, just once more, this examination is intended that we may come to the table with an appreciative joy. Let me explain that rather long word. You know if you come to the communion table saying: 'I do not know whether I have a right to be here', you cannot enjoy yourself. If I were sitting at a man's table, and I said to myself: 'I am afraid I have made a mistake. I do not believe he ever invited me', I should feel very uncomfortable while I was there, and I should be wonderfully glad when the dinner was over. But if, as I sat at the table, I said: 'I know the gentleman invited me. I have his invitation with me and he is smiling upon me, for he is glad that I am here'. That is how I like to feel at the Lord's table – to know, after examination, that I am in my right place. Then I soon forget all about my right to be there and all I think of is that which is on the table, and about my Lord who has invited me, and how I can enjoy the sweetest communion with him, and partake of the dainties which he has put before me.

In short:

I want you, brothers and sisters, to examine yourselves till you come to this conclusion: 'We are not perfect, but we believe in Jesus. We are not yet fully assured, but we have a humble hope in him. We are not the strongest of his warriors, but we have his life in us – we do know him, and trust him'. Then you will feel: 'The good Shepherd feeds the lambs as well as the full-grown sheep of his flock, so we may come to him for all we need'. Then you will have nothing to think about as to yourself, but all you will have to do will be to say: 'My Lord here gives me his flesh to eat, and his blood to drink, after a spiritual fashion. In these outward types, I will now feed upon him. The fact that God took our nature upon himself shall be as food to my soul. The equally blessed fact that being found in fashion as a man, he took my sins upon himself and suffered in my place shall be like generous wine to me. I will drink it down! I will feed upon it! I will live by it!' Then you will have joy and gladness in your soul and this supper will be what it really is – no funeral feast, but a banquet of delight for all the friends of Christ! 'Let a man examine himself' with the view that he may so eat and so drink when he comes to the table of the Lord.[3]

---

[3] Sermon 2699: 'Examination Before Communion' (spurgeongems.org).

I feel sure that Spurgeon has caught the apostle's meaning here. In other words, 1 Corinthians 11:28 makes no contribution whatsoever to making any believer worry about whether or not he is a true believer, no contribution to making him go into introspection, and leading him to depression and lack of assurance.

Appendix 6
2 Peter 1:10

[God's] divine power has given us everything we need for life and godliness through our knowledge of him who called us by his own glory and goodness. Through these he has given us his very great and precious promises, so that through them you may participate in the divine nature and escape the corruption in the world caused by evil desires. For this very reason, make every effort to add to your faith goodness; and to goodness, knowledge; and to knowledge, self-control; and to self-control, perseverance; and to perseverance, godliness; and to godliness, brotherly kindness; and to brotherly kindness, love. For if you possess these qualities in increasing measure, they will keep you from being ineffective and unproductive in your knowledge of our Lord Jesus Christ. But if anyone does not have them, he is nearsighted and blind, and has forgotten that he has been cleansed from his past sins. Therefore, my brothers, be all the more eager to make your calling and election sure. For if you do these things, you will never fall, and you will receive a rich welcome into the eternal kingdom of our Lord and Saviour Jesus Christ (2 Pet. 1:3-11).

The words in question are, of course: 'My brothers, be all the more eager to make your calling and election sure' (2 Pet. 1:10).

What does Peter mean by 'sure'? And 'sure' to whom? He uses *bebaios*, 'stable, fast, firm, sure, trusty', 'certain' (2 Pet. 1:19), 'firm' (Heb. 3:14), 'in force' (Heb. 9:17), 'guaranteed' (Rom. 4:16). The question is, is Peter telling believers that they will know that they are called and elected once they have reached a certain standard of sanctification, and have made sufficient progress? I think not! For a start, I know of no other passage which says it.

So what is Peter saying? It is possible that he is telling believers that the only way to verify, to make sure, confirm and demonstrate to others the reality of their calling and election – the profession of their calling and election – is by their sanctification.[1] That is one possibility.

---

[1] 'What good is it, my brothers, if a man claims to have faith but has no deeds? Can such faith save him?... Faith by itself, if it is not accompanied

Another possibility – and I think most likely right – the thrust of the apostle's words is to do with the perseverance of the saints. Rather like riding a bicycle; if you stop pedalling, in time you come to a standstill and fall off! Keep growing in grace, therefore, until the day you die! This is the way to persevere.

Calvin, commenting on the verse, declared:

It is one proof that we have been really elected, and not in vain called by the Lord, if a good conscience and integrity of life correspond with our profession of faith. And [Peter] infers that there ought to be more labour and diligence, because he had said before that faith ought not to be barren... The meaning then is, labour that you may have it really proved that you have not been called nor elected in vain. At the same time he speaks here of calling as the effect and evidence of election.

What about assurance by sanctification? Calvin again:

Now a question arises: Whether the stability of our calling and election depends on good works, for if it is so, it follows that it depends on us. But the whole Scripture teaches us, first, that God's election is founded on his eternal purpose; and secondly, that calling begins and is completed through his gratuitous goodness... Every [believer] confirms his calling by leading a holy and pious life... The matter stands thus: God effectually calls whom he has pre-ordained to life in his secret counsel before the foundation of the world; and he also carries on the perpetual course of calling through grace alone. But as he has chosen us, and calls us for this end, that we may be pure and spotless in his presence, purity of life is not improperly called the evidence and proof of election, by which the faithful may not only testify to others that they are the children of God, but also confirm themselves in this confidence, in such a manner, however, that they fix their solid foundation on something else.

Calvin was right. Sanctification is both an evidence – a necessary evidence – to others, and a confirmation to the believer, of the reality of his profession. But Peter was not calling the believer to try to reach an elusive assurance by probing his sanctification. He was speaking of a life consistent with his profession, and, above all,

---

by action, is dead... Faith without deeds is useless... A person is justified [in the eyes of others] by what he does and not by faith alone... As the body without the spirit is dead, so faith without deeds is dead' (Jas. 2:14-26).

172

of the necessity of growth in grace and perseverance in the faith. Consistency and growth – both are essential. As the apostle said in his final exhortation in this letter: 'Grow in the grace and knowledge of our Lord and Saviour Jesus Christ' (2 Pet. 3:18).

Sanctification is also, as I have said, the way of perseverance. Now the old (biblical) way of expressing this – 'the perseverance of the saints' – has too often been replaced by the notion of 'the eternal security of believers' or 'once saved, always saved'. These two – perseverance and security – are chalk and cheese. The biblical way of speaking of this matter is in terms of saints (not believers) and their perseverance in godliness. And this is what Peter is calling for here: 'My brothers, be all the more eager to make your calling and election sure' (2 Pet. 1:10). And we do this by producing the works of sanctification which he set out in the verses leading up to his command.

As Calvin went on to say in his comments:

At the same time, this certainty, mentioned by Peter, ought, I think, to be referred to the conscience, as though the faithful acknowledged themselves before God to be chosen and called. But I take it simply of the fact itself, that calling appears as confirmed by this very holiness of life. It may, indeed, be rendered: 'Labour that your calling may become certain...'. The import of what is said is, that the children of God are distinguished from the reprobate by this mark, that they live a godly and a holy life, because this is the design and end of election. Hence it is evident how wickedly some vile unprincipled men prattle, when they seek to make gratuitous election an excuse for all licentiousness; as though... we may sin with impunity, because we have been predestinated to righteousness and holiness!...

[Peter's] purpose was only to show that hypocrites have in them nothing real or solid, and that, on the contrary, they who prove their calling sure by good works are free from the danger of falling, because sure and sufficient is the grace of God by which they are supported. Thus the certainty of our salvation by no means depends on us, as doubtless the cause of it is beyond our limits. But with regard to those who feel in themselves the efficacious working of the Spirit, Peter bids them to take courage as to the future, because the Lord has laid in them the solid foundation of a true and sure calling.

He explains the way or means of persevering, when he says, an entrance shall be ministered to you. The import of the words is this: 'God, by ever supplying you abundantly with new graces, will lead you to his own kingdom'. And this was added, that we may know, that though we have already passed from death into life, yet it is a passage of hope. And as to the fruition of life, there remains for us yet a long journey. In the meantime we are not destitute of necessary helps. Hence Peter obviates a doubt by these words: 'The Lord will abundantly supply your need, until you shall enter into his eternal kingdom'.

I think this is very clear. Calvin did not regard 2 Peter 1:10 as a call to introspection. Not at all! Rather, Peter insists on sanctification as a demonstration and confirmation of inward grace – very much along the lines of Paul to the Ephesians: 'As a prisoner for the Lord, then, I urge you to live a life worthy of the calling you have received... So I tell you this, and insist on it in the Lord, that you must no longer live as the Gentiles do, in the futility of their thinking' (Eph. 4:1,17). And, as he told the Philippians: 'Whatever happens, conduct yourselves in a manner worthy of the gospel of Christ' (Phil. 1:27). And, although I have just quoted it, as Peter urged his readers: 'Grow in the grace and knowledge of our Lord and Saviour Jesus Christ' (2 Pet. 3:18).

Spurgeon, tackling those who think that expressing doubt about oneself is the highest form of spirituality, and those who encourage believers to think it, went for the jugular:

'Make your calling and election sure'. Not towards God, for they are sure to him: make them sure to yourself. Be quite certain of them; be fully satisfied about them. In many of our dissenting places of worship very great encouragement is held out to doubting. A person comes before the pastor, and says: 'Oh! sir, I am so afraid I am not converted; I tremble lest I should not be a child of God. Oh! I fear I am not one of the Lord's elect'. The pastor will put out his hands to him, and say: 'Dear brother, you are all right so long as you can doubt'. Now, I hold, that is altogether wrong. Scripture never says: 'He that doubts shall be saved', but: 'He that believes'. It may be true that the man is in a good state [that is, he is converted]; it may be true that he wants a little comfort; but his doubts are not good things, nor ought we to encourage him in his doubts. Our business is to encourage him out of his doubts, and by the grace of God to urge him to 'give all diligence to make his calling and election sure;' not to doubt it, but to be sure of it.

Spurgeon then directed his attention to the mere professor. Let me stress this – 'the mere professor'; or, in Spurgeon's words, 'the hypocrite'. Spurgeon was clearly directing his remarks to the carnal man, not the doubting true believer:

> Ah! I have heard some hypocritical doubters say: 'Oh! I have had such doubts whether I am the Lord's', and I have thought to myself: 'And so have I very great doubts about you'. I have heard some say they do tremble so because they are afraid they are not the Lord's people; and the lazy fellows sit in their pews on the Sunday, and just listen to the sermon; but they never think of giving diligence, they never do good, perhaps are inconsistent in their lives, and then talk about doubting. It is quite right they should doubt, it is well they should; and if they did not doubt we might begin to doubt for them. Idle men have no right to assurance. The Scripture says: 'Give diligence to make your calling and election sure'.

What about those who say they have heard voices or seen visions?[2]

> Full assurance is an excellent attainment. It is profitable for a man to be certain in this life, and absolutely sure of his own calling and election. But how can he be sure? Now, many of our more ignorant hearers imagine that the only way they have of being assured of their election is by some revelation, some dream, and some mystery. I have enjoyed very hearty laughs at the expense of some people who have trusted in their visions. Really, if you had passed among so many shades of ignorant professing Christians as I have, and had to resolve so many doubts and fears, you would be so infinitely sick of dreams and visions that you would say, as soon as a person began to speak about them: 'Now, do just hold your tongue'. 'Sir', said a woman, 'I saw blue lights in the front parlour when I was in prayer, and I thought I saw the Saviour in the corner, and I said to myself: "I am safe"'... And yet there are tens of thousands of people in every part of the country, and members too of Christians bodies, who have no better ground for their belief that they are called and elected, than some vision equally ridiculous, or the equally absurd hearing of a voice. A young woman came to me some time ago; she wanted to join the church, and when I asked her how she knew herself to be converted, she said she was down at the bottom of the garden, and she thought she heard a voice, and she thought she saw something up in the clouds that said to her so-and-so. 'Well', I said to her, 'that thing may have been the means of doing good to you, but if you put any trust in it, it is all over with you'. A dream, yes, and a vision, may often bring men to Christ. I have known many who have been brought to him by them,

---

[2] This, of course, is a million miles away from the witness of the Spirit.

beyond a doubt, though it has been mysterious to me how it was. But when men bring these forward as a proof of their conversion, there is the mistake, because you may see fifty thousand dreams and fifty thousand visions, and you may be a fool for all that, and all the bigger sinner for having seen them.

Spurgeon turned to the scriptural way:

There is better evidence to be had than all this: 'Give diligence to make your calling and election sure'. 'How, then', says one, 'am I to make my calling and election sure?'

In an extended passage, Spurgeon then spelled out the marks of grace – the things the apostle listed in verses 5 to 8; in other words, practical godliness, growing in grace, sanctification. This is the only way to prove to others that we are converted. A man may profess what he will, but his life must be consistent with it:

When you have got all these, then you will know your calling and election, and just in proportion as you practice these heavenly rules of life, in this heavenly manner, will you come to know that you are called and that you are elect. But by no other means can you attain to a knowledge of that, except by the witness of the Spirit, bearing witness with your spirit that you are born of God, and then witnessing in your conscience that you are not what you were, but are a new man in Christ Jesus, and are therefore called and therefore elected.

A man over there says he is elect. He gets drunk. Yes, you are elect by the devil, sir; that is about your only election. Another man says: 'Blessed be God, I don't care about evidences a bit; I am not so legal as you are!' No, I dare say you are not, but you have no great reason to bless God about it, for, my dear friend, unless you have these evidences of a new birth take heed to yourself. 'God is not mocked: whatsoever a man sows, that shall he also reap'. 'Well', says another, 'but I think that doctrine of election is a very licentious doctrine'. Think on as long as you please, but please to bear me witness that as I have preached it today there is nothing licentious about it. Very likely you are licentious, and you would make the doctrine licentious, if you believed it, but 'to the pure all things are pure'. He who receives God's truth in his heart does not often pervert it and turn aside from it unto wicked ways. No man, let me repeat, has any right to believe himself called, unless his life be in the main consistent with his vocation, and he walk worthy of that whereunto he is called. Out upon an election that lets you live in sin! Away with it! Away with it! That was never the design of God's word; and it never was the doctrine of Calvinists either. Though we have been lied against and our teachings perverted, we have always stood by this – that good works, though they do not procure nor in any degree merit salvation, yet are the necessary evidences of salvation, and unless they be in men the soul is still dead, uncalled and unrenewed. The nearer you live to Christ, the more you imitate him, the more your life is conformed to him, and the more simply you hang upon him by faith, the more certain you may be of your election in Christ and of your calling by his Holy Spirit. May the Holy One of Israel give you the sweet assurance of grace, by affording you 'tokens for good' in the graces which he enables you to manifest.[3]

In other words, Peter is not calling believers to a harrowing self-examination over a considerable period of time (verse 8) to obtain assurance. Rather, he is calling them to be sanctified, in order to demonstrate, to verify and to confirm the reality of their experience of the gospel to others, and to make sure they, themselves, persevere to the end. Paul, at the close of his life, could declare; 'The time has come for my departure. I have fought the good fight, I have finished the race, I have kept the faith' (2 Tim. 4:6-7). Remember Christ's words to the church in Smyrna: 'Be faithful, even to the point of death' (Rev. 2:10). 'The perseverance of the saints' means what it says on the tin! And being assured certainly helps in that essential perseverance! Living a life of fear (what a travesty of the gospel!) – fear under the law for sanctification, fear under sanctification by the law for assurance – has nothing – nothing – to do with the gospel as revealed in the New Testament.

---

[3] Sermon number 123.

Source List

Abrams, M.H., (General Editor): *The Norton Anthology of English Literature*, Vol.2, W.W.Norton & Company, New York, 1979.

Atherstone, Andrew and Jones, David Ceri (eds.): *Engaging With Martyn Lloyd-Jones: The Life and Legacy of 'the Doctor'*, Apollos, Nottingham, 2011.

Bauckham, Richard: 'Adding to the Church – During the Early American Period' in *Adding to the Church*, The Westminster Conference, 1973.

Bavinck, Herman: *Reformed Dogmatics*, Vol.4, Baker Academic, Grand Rapids, 2008.

Baxter, Richard: *The Autobiography of Richard Baxter*, J.M.Dent & Sons Ltd., London, 1931.

Beeke, Joel R.: *The Quest for Full Assurance: The Legacy of Calvin and His Successors*, The Banner of Truth Trust, Edinburgh, 1999.

Beeke, Joel R.: 'Martin Luther on Assurance' (biblicalstudies.org.uk).

Brooks, Thomas: *Heaven on Earth: A Serious Discourse, Touching a Well-Grounded Assurance* in *The Works of Thomas Brooks*, Vol.2, The Banner of Truth Trust, Edinburgh, 1980 (also in paperback, 1961).

Calvin, *Commentaries*.

Chrisco, Gerald L.: 'Theology of Assurance within the Marrow Controversy' (rts.edu).

Coffey, John: *John Goodwin and the Puritan Revolution...*, The Boydell Press, Woodbridge, 2006.

Dabney, Robert L.: *Discussions: Evangelical and Theological*, Vol.1, The Banner of Truth Trust, Edinburgh, 1967.

Dabney, Robert L.: *Systematic Theology*, The Banner of Truth Trust, Edinburgh, 1985.

Darby, J.N.: *Synopsis of the Books of the Bible*, Vol.4, third edition (revised), G.Morrish, London.

Dunn, James D.G.: *Baptism in the Holy Spirit*, Westminster Press, Philadelphia, 1970.

Dunn, James D.G: *Jesus and the Spirit...*, Westminster Press, Philadelphia, 1975.

Dunn, James D.G.: 'Spirit Speech: Reflections on Romans 8:12-17' in Soderlund, Sven K. & Wright, N.T. (eds.): *Romans & The People of God...*, William B.Eerdmans Publishing Company, Grand Rapids, 1999.

Eaton, Michael A.: *A Theology of Encouragement*, Paternoster Press, Carlisle, 1995.

Eaton, Michael: *1,2,3 John*, Christian Focus Publications, Fearn, 1996.

Eaton, Michael, A.: *No Condemnation: A Theology of Assurance of Salvation*, Piquant Editions, Carlisle, 2013.

Edwards, Jonathan: *Diary*, in *The Works of Jonathan Edwards, Revised and Corrected by Edward Hickman*, Vol.1, The Banner of Truth Trust, Edinburgh, 1974.

Edwards, Jonathan: *The Religious Affections...*, American Tract Society, New York.

Edwards, Jonathan: *The Works of Jonathan Edwards*, Vol.1 and Vol.2 (hopefaithprayer.com).

Erskine, Ralph: *Select Sermons of Ralph Erskine*, Old Paths Gospel Press, Choteau.

Evans, Eifion: *Daniel Rowland...*, The Banner of Truth Trust, Edinburgh, 1985.

Fee, Gordon D.: *The First Epistle to the Corinthians*, William B.Eerdmans Publishing Company, Grand Rapids, reprinted 1991.

Fee, Gordon D.: *God's Empowering Spirit...*, Hendrickson Publishers, Peabody, 1995.

Gay, David H.J.: *Particular Redemption and the Free Offer*, Brachus, Biggleswade, 2008.

Gay, David H.J.: *Infant Baptism Tested*, Brachus, Biggleswade, 2009.

Gay, David H.J.: *Baptist Sacramentalism: A Warning to Baptists*, Brachus, Biggleswade, 2011.

Gay, David H.J.: *Christ is All: No Sanctification by the Law*, Brachus, Wilstead, 2013.

Gay, David H.J.: *Sanctification in Galatians*, Brachus, Wilstead, 2013.

Gay, David H.J.: *Eternal Justification: Gospel Preaching to Sinners Marred by Hyper-Calvinism*, Brachus, Wilstead, 2013.

Gay, David H.J.: *Four 'Antinomians' Tried and Vindicated...*, Brachus, Wilstead, 2014.

Gay, David H.J.: *The Glorious New-Covenant Ministry: Its Basis and Practice*, Brachus, Wilstead, 2014.

Gay, David H.J.: *The Hinge in Romans 1 – 8: A critique of N.T.Wright's view of Baptism and Conversion*, Brachus, Wilstead, 2014.

Gilbert, Martin: *Winston Churchill: The Wilderness Years*, Book Club Associates, London, 1981.

Gill, John: *Commentary*.

Gillies, John: *Memoirs of The Life of... George Whitefield...*, New Haven, 1812.

Gosden, J.H.: *What Gospel Standard Baptists Believe*, Gospel Standard Societies, Chippenham, 1993.

Gospel Hymns, The Strict and Particular Baptist Society, Robert Stockwell, London, 1915.

Hall, D.D., in Hall, David D. (ed): *The Antinomian Controversy, 1636-1638: A Documentary History*, Duke University Press, (2nd revised edition), 1990.

Hammond, William: 'A Preface, Giving Some Account of a Weak Faith, and a Full Assurance of Faith; and Briefly Stating the Doctrine of Sanctification; and Showing a Christian's Completeness, Perfection, and Happiness in Christ' in *Psalms, Hymns and Spiritual Songs*, W.Strahan, London, 1745.

Hawker, Robert: *Commentary* (studylight.org).

Henry, Matthew: *Commentary*.

Hodge, Charles: *A Commentary on the Second Epistle to the Corinthians*, The Banner of Truth Trust, London, 1963.

Hodges, Zane C.: 'Assurance: Of the Essence of Saving Faith' (faithalone.org).

Hulse, Erroll: *The Believer's Experience*, Carey Publications, Haywards Heath, 1977.

Kevan, Ernest F.: *The Saving Work of the Holy Spirit*, Pickering & Inglis, Ltd., London, 1953.

Kimnach, Wilson H., Minkema, Kenneth P. and Sweeney, Douglas A.: *The Sermons of Jonathan Edwards: A Reader*, Yale University, 1999.

Lloyd-Jones, D.Martyn: *Romans: An Exposition of Chapter 1. The Gospel of God*, The Banner of Truth Trust, Edinburgh, 1985.

Lloyd-Jones, D.Martyn: *Romans: An Exposition of Chapter 8:5-17. The Sons of God*, The Banner of Truth Trust, Edinburgh, 1974.

Source List

Lloyd-Jones, D.Martyn: *An Exposition of Ephesians 1:1-23. God's Ultimate Purpose*, The Banner of Truth Trust, Edinburgh, 1978.

Lloyd-Jones, D.Martyn: *The Christian Warfare: Ephesians 6:10-13*, The Banner of Truth Trust, Edinburgh, 1976.

Lloyd-Jones, D.Martyn: 'Sandemanianism' in *The Puritans: Their Origins and Successors*, The Banner of Truth Trust, Edinburgh, 1987.

Lloyd-Jones, D.Martyn: 'Howell Harris and Revival' in *The Puritans: Their Origins and Successors*, The Banner of Truth Trust, Edinburgh, 1987.

Lloyd-Jones, D.Martyn: *Preaching and Preachers*, Hodder and Stoughton, London, 1971.

Lloyd-Jones, D.Martyn: *Joy Unspeakable*, Kingsway, Eastbourne, 1984.

Longenecker, R.N.: *Galatians*, Word Books, Dallas, 1990.

Macarthur, John: 'Why Christians Lack Assurance' (gty.org).

Moo, Douglas J.: *The Epistle to the Romans*, William B.Eerdmans, Grand Rapids, 1996.

Morey, Robert A.: 'Knowing You Are Saved: Part 4' (davidsonpress.com).

Murray, Iain H.: 'Assurance of Salvation' in *The Old Evangelicalism...*, The Banner of Truth Trust, Edinburgh, 2005.

Murray, John: 'The Assurance of Faith' in *Collected Writings...*, Vol.2, The Banner of Truth Trust, Edinburgh, 1977.

Neuman, H.Terris: 'Paul's Appeal to the Experience of the Spirit in Galatians 3:1-5: Christian Experience as Defined by the Cross and Effected by the Spirit', *Journal of Pentecostal Theology*, Issue 9, Sheffield Academic Press, Sheffield, 1996.

Owen, John: *A Practical Exposition upon Psalm 130...* in *The Works of John Owen*, Vol.6, The Banner of Truth Trust, London, 1966.

Packer, J.I.: *Keep in Step With the Spirit*, Inter-Varsity Press, Leicester, 1984.

Packer, J.I.: 'The Witness of the Spirit in Puritan Thought' in *Among God's Giants...*, Kingsway Publications, Eastbourne, 1991.

Pink., A.W.: 'Assurance' (spureongems.org).

Piper, John: 'Helping People Have the Assurance of Salvation' (desiringgod.org).

Piper, John: 'The Agonizing Problem of the Assurance of Salvation' (desiringgod.org).

Pratt, John H. (ed.): The Thoughts of the Evangelical Leaders..., The Banner of Truth Trust, Edinburgh, 1978.

Reformation Today.

Sawyer, M.James: 'Some Thoughts On Lordship Salvation' (bible.org).

Stibbs, A.M. and Packer. J.I.: *The Spirit Within You: The Church's Neglected Possession*, Hodder and Stoughton, London, 1967.

Stott, John: *The Message of Romans...*, Inter-Varsity Press, Leicester, 1994.

Thayer, Joseph Henry: *A Greek-English Lexicon of the New Testament*, Baker Book House, Grand Rapids, Ninth Printing 1991.

Tozer, A.W.: *Gems from Tozer*, Christian Publications, Camp Hill, 1979.

Tyler, Bennet and Bonar, Andrew: *Asahel Nettleton: Life and Labours*, The Banner of Truth Trust, Edinburgh, 1975.

Tyndale, William: *An Answer to Sir Thomas More's Dialogue: The Supper...*, edited by Henry Walter, Vol.44, The Parker Society, The University Press, Cambridge, 1850.

Whitefield, George: *Sermons on Important Subjects by... George Whitefield*, Thomas Tegg, & Son, London, 1838.

Wilkin, Bob: 'Assurance by Inner Witness? Romans 8:16' (faithalone.org).

Wright, N.T.: 'Believing and Belonging' (ntwrightpage.com).

Printed in Great Britain
by Amazon.co.uk, Ltd.,
Marston Gate.

6533395R00109